Possessing

THE Seven

Mountains

Possessing

THE *Seven*

Mountains

Written By:
Joe Paul

Publisher:
Daughters of Distinction

"Possessing the Seven Mountains
Published by Daughters of Distinction

PO Box 9001
Silver Springs, MD 20916 USA

Cover Design and Layout: Ebony Richardson
Editorial: Mia Grice-McGee

FOREWORD

When I met Apostle Joe Paul, our meeting was ordained by God and the profundity of our shared destiny was inescapable. It is rare that one is able to sit at the feet of a true man of God. We have become more than friends, we are brothers. When he informed me that he was going to write a new book entitled, "Possessing the Seven Mountains, 7 Spheres of Influence", I was overjoyed. My excitement was due largely to the fact that I have had the awesome privilege of enjoying some of his previous works. In particular, the book entitled, "THE POWER AND INFLUENCE OF AL-TARS." I have waited with baited breath for the next project that he would masterfully craft. Thankfully, the wait was brief considering the vast amounts of research, recall and revelation needed to complete such a task.

From the very first chapter entitled, "THE MOUNTAIN ABOVE THE MOUNTAINS" where Apostle Joe adeptly elucidates his readers on the polygenesis of the seven mountains. He goes on to set the thematic foundation by the placing at the federal head of his treatise the principle of the Lord's House being the "Eighth Mountain." He goes on to intimate that the conceptualization of the seven mountains can only be fully imbibed by understanding or rather standing under this irrefutable fact.

I am encouraged that he wisely sets out from the first chapter to the end of the book instructing his readers to pray in a specific manner using prayer points for the purpose of attaining sovereign authority over each of the "Seven Mountains."

In the final chapter of his masterpiece, Apostle Joe warns us about "The Neglected Conflict." This is a fitting resolve of his treatise chiefly because of the compromising constitution of today's body of Christ. He confers to his readers the knowledge of the reality of the ongoing battle between the Kingdom of Darkness and the Kingdom of Light.

I am graciously in the Master's debt for allowing me to be in Apostle Joe Paul's sphere of influence and he in mine. Once in a decade a work of this magnitude comes to the forefront; as such I, with singleness of mind and without hesitation implore you to add this book to your must read list.

Apostle Timothy R.S. Weathers
Senior Pastor
RHEMA International Ministries

TABLE OF CONTENTS

Preface   9

Acknowledgements   11

Chapter One:
The Mountain Above the Mountains   13

Chapter Two:
Understanding the Foundation of the Mountains   22

Chapter Three: The Neglected Conflict   31

Chapter Four: Threshing Process   40

Chapter Five: The Selection Process   48

Chapter Six: Remnant Generation   56

Chapter Seven: Understanding the Mandate   62

Chapter Eight: Training and Preparation   70

Chapter Nine: Survey & Investigation   81

Chapter Ten: Contest on the Mountains   91

Chapter Eleven: Possession and Dominion   97

Chapter Twelve:
Possession and Dominion 2   108

Chapter Thirteen:
The Rod of Zion and the Team   116

Chapter Fourteen:
Strategic High Level Spiritual Warfare   122

Epilogue   130

About The Author

PREFACE

The seven mountain philosophy is an understanding from the Holy Spirit unto the Church, which tends to bring a renewed emphasis on the gospel of the kingdom. These emphases are firstly, on the doctrine of separation of secularity from spirituality and secondly, the dichotomy between the clergy and laity, all must be jettisoned by the Church, now as never. The whole universe and indeed the planet earth are spiritual entities. While I can adduce that the era of clergy-laity divide has ended.

These naiveties have given the enemy greater concessions and occasions to perpetuate his stronghold on the earth. It has given strength to the kingdom of darkness to anoint strong forces that fought godliness and entrenched darkness in the public places and institutions called the Seven Mountains. Somehow, a carnally orchestrated assessment may tend to look as if GOD and his fundamental principles on the earth in some nations and mountains are defeated.

Understanding the role of the Church to her nation will reposition the Church towards a return to national revivals that will give birth to eventual national transformation and consequent repossession of the Seven Mountains of influence. Since, we did not heed the voice of the LORD as did the young Israeli nation in their then newly repossessed land of Promise.

We have left in our territories against the counsel of GOD, the remnants of the Hittites, the Girgasites, the Amorites, the Canaanites, the Perizzites, Hivites and the Jebusites. These remnants (some of them giants) became stronger. They did not only rebel against Israel, but began to oppress them in their own (promised) land.

Understanding and knowing how to depose the enemies from the Seven Mountains, how to recover the unconquered territories and establish the principles of the kingdom of GOD is the mainstay and logic in this treatise. It is possible! GOD did it in sundry times and in diverse ways. He is doing it now and will continue to that whenever He sees a willing vessel.

We need a reconfiguration of our mind from the old mindset. We need to see the Mountains as opportunities to prove the possibilities of total takeover not opposition to the Church. This is the era of exploits by the five-fold ministry to showcase the unsearchable greatness of His Power. May GOD find you as willing vessels in His hand.

Joe Paul

ACKNOWLEDGEMENTS

My deepest appreciation to the Almighty GOD, who gave me the inspiration to write this book.

My wonderful wife who works tirelessly as an engineer and has proved that GOD is in and he owns the marketplaces. She took the message of responsibilities of possessing the Seven Mountains to her office. She has proved that total takeover is possible. She has always been reminding me of the need to finish the suspended scripts.

Great thanks to my two lovely children, whose constant interferences have always made me to ponder deeply on the book.

I cannot thank Apostle Trena Stephenson of Maryland (USA) enough for accepting to publish this book, but also to bankroll the costs and also market the book. May the good LORD who brought us together bless you richly.

Also, Dr. Becky and Apostle Paul Murray of Woodstock, Virginia. They put together the international conference in Edinburg, Virginia that gave birth to this book.

The teachings of these great men of GOD from Nigeria made and are making great differences in the marketplaces: Pa Emeka Nwankpa, Pastor Victor Uchegbulam, Pastor

David Ogbueli and Professor Vincent Anigbogu they have been great source of inspiration to I and many others. I appreciate you all.

And last, but not least, special thanks to Apostle Timothy R.S. Weathers for contributing the Foreword.

May the LORD depend on you all for the on-going contest and transformation on Seven Mountains.

Joe Paul

Chapter One

THE MOUNTAIN ABOVE THE MOUNTAINS

The Polygenesis of Seven Mountains

The awareness and the expository teachings on Seven Mountains of Influence or society has ignited a lot of positive inspirations in the body of CHRIST. For more than four decades, now and will continue to do so till the Church of GOD comes to the fullness of her capacity; both in words and in actions. This capacity will be geared towards possessing the seven mountains.

The precepts and the insights came into the Church through a threshold of polygenesis. Simultaneously, GOD raised many apostles, prophets and teachers from the churches in Europe, America, Africa and Asia with different topics and wisdom geared towards transformation in the market place called Seven Mountains.

The origin of these concepts is traceable to Bill Bright, the founder of Campus Crusade, and Loren Cunningham, the founder of Youth With a Mission (YWAM). Ever since 1975 when this teachings came into limelight, many great men of GOD have risen and delivered thought provoking teachings that tend to prepare the unprepared Church for a great exploit and eventual takeover of the gates and the mountains of nations.

The divine aim is to equip, impart and disciple a kingdom-conscious people for their respective national transformation and eventual global wealth transfer. The mountain of religion, which has not been recognized as the focal and decisive mountain up until now; should not only be seen, but must be known as the chief of all the mountains.

In categorizing the Seven Mountains, the concept is that the mountains of influence are seven in number. Cartographically, the mountain of the LORD's house, which the Church as a religious mountain represents, is seen from the under mentioned opening text as number eight. It stands higher than all the mountains and it has a domineering influence above the other seven mountains and other hills. The efficacy of this mountain must be recognized as the most essential and influential gateway to the other mountains.

These Seven Mountains are named:

1. Religion
2. Politics
3. Media
4. Entertainment and sports
5. Education
6. Economy/Business
7. Family

The Mountain above the Mountains
In these opening texts:
Isaiah 2:2-3(KJV)
>   *²And it shall come to pass in the last days, that the mountain of the LORD's house shall be established in the top of the mountains, and shall be exalted above the hills; ³and all nations shall flow unto it. And many people shall go and say, Come ye, and let us go up to the mountain of the LORD, to the house of the God of Jacob; and he will teach us of his ways, and we will walk in his paths: for out of Zion shall go forth the law,*

and the word of the LORD from Jerusalem.
Micah 4:1(KJV)

¹But in the last days it shall come to pass, <u>that the mountain of the house of the LORD shall be established in the top of the mountains, and it shall be exalted above the hills</u>; and people shall flow unto it.

Mountain Number Eight

Consider the import of the underlined words in the above quoted scriptures; the **mountain** (singular), which will be established on top of the **mountains** (plural). And above all, this emerging mountain will be exalted above the **hills** also in plural. These phrases, '**on top of the mountains**' and '**on top of the hills**' are profound indications that the emerging mountain is the Church.

The last sentence as highlighted in verse three, GOD reassured us that laws and edicts for the transformation will come from Zion which the Church represents. The manifestation is going to be unprecedented. That all nations will see it and flow to it means that it will bring mass scale repentance and conversion.

These text, underscores the whole heavenly cardinal points agenda that the current move will indeed reposition the Church for a total takeover. This mountain is the basis and concept of this entire treatise. This mountain indeed is a spiritual move of GOD. It represents the advancement of the kingdom of GOD in every sphere of influence. The house of the LORD is the Church also known as, Mount Zion. The book of Isaiah buttresses this fact. **Isaiah 56:7 (NKJV):** *For my house shall be called a house of prayer for all nations.*

The Mountain as the Move of GOD

This mountain is symbolic as the rock which was revealed to Nebuchadnezzar and as interpreted by

Daniel. It is that rock that was not cut with human hands but crushed the existing statue and became a great and everlasting mountain that filled the whole earth. This statue which the rock crushed represents the existing negative world views, mindsets, the so-called new age movements and the new world orders that are being designed, crafted and advanced without GOD.

Daniel 2:34-35 (NIV)
34While you were watching, a rock was cut out, but not by human hands. It struck the statue on its feet of iron and clay and smashed them. 35Then the iron, the clay, the bronze, the silver and the gold were broken to pieces at the same time and became like chaff on a threshing floor in the summer. The wind swept them away without leaving a trace. But the rock that struck the statue became a huge mountain and filled the whole earth.

That the rock became a huge mountain and filled the whole world is indicating that the Church, which no man formed or established, will definitely overcome the existing so-called super structures of nations. The LORD has promised '*I will build my Church; and the gates of hell shall not prevail against it*' (Matt. 16:18). He shed His blood for the Church. He is building His Church. The Church is actually not a building, but a people. The called-out ones '*the Ecclesia*'.

Consider the import of this phrase in the following scriptures: 'In the time of those kings--.' This is the time of those kings. Though men have established empires, organizations, multinationals and great institutions without GOD, though they have the strength of iron and steel, yet JEHOVAH YAHWEH SABAOTH the LORD of hosts has determined their collapse. He is raising an army that will midwife the emerging new kingdom order.

Daniel 2:44-45 (NIV)
44In the time of those kings, the God of heaven will set up a
kingdom that will never be destroyed, nor will it be left to
another people. It will crush all those kingdoms and bring
them to an end, but it will itself endure forever. 45This is the
meaning of the vision of the rock cut out of a mountain, but not
by human hands — a rock that broke the iron, the bronze, the
clay, the silver and the gold to pieces.

Transformation on the Mountains

The book of Obadiah stated that in mount Zion, which the Church stands for. Their deliverance will come to the called-out ones (the Ecclesia). These special breed of people, after being delivered/released, will supervise the transformation on the mountains. That means that there will be transformation in and from the Church. This transformation will be all inclusive. It will transcend through the mind, spirit, soul and body.

Obadiah 1:17 (KJV)
17 But upon mount Zion shall be deliverance, and there shall be
holiness; and the house of Jacob shall possess their possessions.

Furthermore, these deliverances that will occur in the Mount Zion will prepare the Ecclesia for the eventual great harvest.

Obadiah 1:21 (NAS)
21The deliverers will ascend Mount Zion
To judge the mountain of Esau, And the kingdom will be the
LORD'S.

This mountain has been prophesied by Prophet Obadiah that this class of emerging force will be known as deliverers. They will firstly ascend the mountain of the

Church (Zion) through the mountain of Religion. They will establish rulership over the mountain of the heathen and eventually dedicate the mountains to the LORD.

In the following scriptures, GOD mentioned the nations that must be deposed. They have established their kingdom order, structures and infrastructures on their respective mountains. GOD has promised to use the Church to depose them and repossess the mountains.

The Emergence and Certainty of the Mountains
Deuteronomy 7:1 (NKJV)
¹When the LORD your God brings you into the land which you go to possess, and has cast out many nations before you, the Hittites and the Girgashites and the Amorites and the Canaanites and the Perizzites and the Hivites and the Jebusites, seven nations greater and mightier than you.

Firstly, GOD did not give Israel an uninhabited virgin forest. He gave them the lands which were being inhabited by not just a people but **nations stronger and mightier than they were**. Secondly, the scripture did not state 'If the LORD your GOD will bring you', but it stated When the LORD your GOD brings you into the land. There was, there is, and will forever be an unconditional bond that the LORD and His people are on course towards possessing the nations.

The Foundations of the Mountains
Where did GOD promise to give them? He gave them a place He vowed to Abraham with a covenant that his children will inherit forever. A place which GOD gave them has a foundation. He was the architect of the foundation.

Hebrew 11:10 (NIV)

¹⁰For he was looking forward to the city with foundations, whose architect and builder is GOD.

In spite of GOD's foundations there, other nations were there building their own idolatrous and atheistic foundations. But GOD had already given a time frame for the total fall of that system and eventual reestablishment of His kingdom at an appointed time. The set time was four hundred years or four generations. (Gen. 15:13-16). Why should GOD wait for a four hundred year period before the fulfillment of those promises? I have seen only one reason; those seven nations were dwelling there committing abominations and iniquities.

The righteous long suffering GOD would want to wait until their iniquities runs its full course. Then, GOD will be justified when He shall judge. Many nations are gradually eroding and degrading into the fullness of the measure of their iniquities. The architects are confidently satisfied of the durability of their global superfluous atheistic system. These are vain imaginations. GOD is bringing a great shaking to every system. Since GOD's four generations means four hundred years. Many mountains are overripe for the inversion and some are closer to the time and season of the eventual and expected visitations.

Genesis 15:13-16 (NIV)
¹³ Then the LORD said to him, "Know for certain that your descendants will be strangers in a country not their own, and they will be enslaved and mistreated <u>four hundred years</u>. ¹⁴But I will punish the nation they serve as slaves, and afterward they will come out with great possessions. ¹⁵You, however, will go to your ancestors in peace and be buried at a good old age. 16 In the fourth generation your descendants will come back here, for the sin of the Amorites has not yet reached its full measure."

Let the occupants of our mountains know and

understand that the time of the full measures of their iniquities has come. As GOD finished His transactions with Abram on the (promised) land; he allowed the Church to go into exile until the appointed time. When the time came for the dispossession of the occupants, it was GOD who led the overthrow.

The Expected Shaking of the Mountains and their Structures

Haggai 2:21-22 (KJV)

[21]...I will shake the heavens and the earth; [22] And I will overthrow the throne of kingdoms, and I will destroy the strength of the kingdoms of the heathen; and I will overthrow the chariots, and those that ride in them; and the horses and their riders shall come down, everyone by the sword of his brother.

Haggai 2:23 (NIV)

[23] " 'On that day,' declares the Lord Almighty, 'I will take you, my servant Zerubbabel son of Shealtiel,' declares the Lord, 'and I will make you like my signet ring, for I have chosen you,' declares the Lord Almighty."

GOD's agenda in the new dispensation is to bring a great shaking upon all the negative godless structures of the nations, thrones and powers of all the secular systems that are built without GOD. In addition, there will be utter confusion in the camp of the enemy which will culminate in their fighting one another.

The text ended with a statement, which implies that in the midst of the shaking, GOD will elect prophetic seeds as leaders extraordinaire. This company of leaders will have the calling and anointing of Zerubbabel. These ones will be the LORD's Signet Ring, which will be a symbol of GOD's mandate. They will make irrevocable decrees that can never be altered.

In Nigeria, GOD has started a great and wonderful harvest amongst the traditional thrones. GOD raised a young articulate and humble prophetic seed. He received of the LORD a commission to gather together the kings in Nigeria. He started with them the Fellowship of Christian Traditional Rulers of Nigeria Rulers (FECTRON). Whosoever that encounters the fellowship has always humbled him/herself in awe of HIM. Recently, it has become an African continental affair. Kings of other nations have begun to desire to emulate the awesome harvest of kings in Nigeria; someone received the vision and ran with it. What have you received from the LORD and refused to run with? Behold this is the time. It cannot be in another time neither with another person.

Prayer Points

Pray these prayers: My LORD and my GOD you are my Father, you created me in your own image and likeness, help me to function effectively on the mountain of my calling in JESUS name.

- LORD, establish my feet in my own mountain and to make impact in my generation.

- Oh GOD, make me to be relevant on my mountain of endeavor.

- My FATHER, cause my voice to be heard on the seven mountains.

- Oh LORD, reveal to me the constituents in the foundation of the mountains.

Chapter Two

UNDERSTANDING THE FOUNDATION OF THE MOUNTAINS

The Mountains Must Be Investigated

In the just concluded chapter one, Abraham was searching for a city with foundations whose maker and builder is GOD. Just as the history of the foundation of United States of America was traceable to the remnant migrant puritans of the European extraction who were searching for a safe haven to establish real worship of the LORD. This puritans who were born out of horrible persecution in Europe, managed to escape to this new world that is today a great place.

The various covenants, dedications and declarations to establish pure and undefiled piety will continue to be a memorial before GOD. It doesn't matter what the gay movement, Freemasonry and Illuminati organizations are doing to rewrite the history of the Americas. All their grand designs to ostracize the living GOD secularize America and promote satanic worship. It should be known that the foundations of the LORD remain sure. GOD understands the foundations and the sacrifices of the founding fathers. He will not leave nor forsake His people.

2 Timothy 2:19 (KJV)   22

¹⁹Nevertheless the foundation of God standeth sure, having this seal, The Lord knoweth them that are his. And, Let everyone that nameth the name of Christ depart from iniquity.

I have known and encountered situations in personal lives, families, communities, and companies that were besieged by unprecedented crisis. The crisis was so grave that it appeared as it has defied every conceivable solution. I have been involved in my city in dealing with a multinational organization which was known to have oppressed its host communities. In prospecting of minerals in Africa, the host communities are given certain privileges. In turn, this company will collude with a few chiefs and elites give them a certain percentage of the stipulated cost of the social amenities as prescribed by MOU.

This company will depend on their sorceries and sacrifices to suppress any opposing voice from the communities. Government agencies, like the law enforcement agencies, will be provided by covert action to protect the companies from any violent incursion from the communities. The LORD led a few of us who began intercession and some prophetic prayers against the company. Within a short period, many things began to unfold. These companies and government have since paid and will still pay huge sum of monies as compensation to many communities. The foundation they laid at the beginning was wrong, GOD raised those who came and dealt with the foundations and positive developments started.

In some lives, families and communities, there are certain spiritual transactions that were set in place from the inception. Some of them are covenant promises, dedication and consulting of with doctors for the so-called good of the beneficiary. There could be peace at certain time but there is always a time of shaking. This shaking will give birth to some militating crisis. Wrong foundations are in many occasions the reasons for certain untold tribulations. We need to take a critical look on how our live, families and institution started. What were the motives and also certain positive and negative transactions, which took place at any stage of development?

The Foundation of Nations and Mountains

The LORD has and knows the foundation of nations in His file. Many nations have risen in sundry times and seasons. One thing made a nation or a kingdom great in their season but another thing brings them down. All the great ancient empires that existed and are no more were all brought down on the grounds of their iniquities.

To take over nations and kingdoms, we need to know and understand the various levels of their foundations. This will equip us to conceive the strategies towards taking over the mountains. Before the LORD gave the Israelis the Promised Land, he led Abraham to know that the iniquities of the Amorites have not yet got to the brim of their cup. At the expiration of the appointed time, he made Moses to understand that their iniquities were getting closer to their full measures.

Genesis 15:16 (NIV)
[16]"In the fourth generation your descendants will come back here, for the sin of the Amorites has not yet reached its full measure."

The Cup of "Iniquities are Being Filled

The nations of the earth are busy filling up the cups of their iniquities. This is the generation which GOD has appointed to visit. The iniquities of the Amorite kingdoms are made manifest in all the mountains of nations. GOD, no doubt, is in a hurry to raise an Eliakhim company who will recover the lost glory of the lost territories and institutions worldwide.

The Judgments on the Mountains and Their Inhabitants
Isaiah 22:20-24 (NIV)

20"In that day I will summon my servant, Eliakim son of Hilkiah. I will clothe him with your robe and fasten your sash around him and hand your authority over to him. He will be a father to those who live in Jerusalem and to the house of Judah. I will drive him like a peg into a firm place; he will be a seat of honor for the house of his father. All the glory of his family will hang on him: its offspring and offshoots- all its lesser vessels, from the bowls to all the jars."

Many world class universities and institutions of higher learning, mostly in Europe and America today were originally designed to train and disciple men and women with biblical ideologies. As time passed by, from the age of industrial revolution to this present age; the world has degenerated through many generations of serious and gradual erosion into godlessness. GOD's prophetic agenda is to raise a people who will understand by the book as did Daniel, the events that gave rise to desolations of many generations.

The earth is on the verge of mourning because of the iniquities of men. Leviticus 18:1-24 stated the nature of sins that could defile the land and cause its inhabitants to be vomited.

The Expected Collapse
Leviticus 18:25 (NKJV)

25For the land is defiled; therefore I visit the punishment of its iniquity upon it, and the land vomits out its inhabitants.

The entire Chapter 18 of the Book of Leviticus deals extensively with sexual perversions and it concluded that those transgressions are among the sins that defile the land thereby causing it to vomit its inhabitants. Today, the proponents of these perversions have hijacked almost all the mountains and are busy rewriting and desecrating the divine injunctions.

The Causes of Desolations of Many Generations

The LORD gave me an understanding sometimes ago, that the major reason for the infamous **Trans-Atlantic** slave trade was as a result of massive bloodshed, idolatry, witchcraft and sexual perversion of Africans in their own land. Owing to these, the land became sick and began to vomit its inhabitants. Consequently, these drew merchants from the first world with slave ships into Africa to import those that were being vomited by the lands. As soon as, much human capitals were carried out by being vomited. GOD arranged and exported burdened missionaries afterwards with the gospel back to Africa.

The next scripture states that the LORD also brought out a nine count charge for a people on a land and declared:

Hosea 4:1-3 (NIV)
¹Hear the word of the LORD, you Israelites,
because the LORD has a charge to bring
against you who live in the land:
"There is no faithfulness, no love,
no acknowledgment of God in the land.
²There is only cursing, lying and murder,
stealing and adultery;
they break all bounds,
and bloodshed follows bloodshed.
³Because of this the land mourns,
and all who live in it waste away;
the beasts of the field, the birds in the sky
and the fish in the sea are swept away.

These charges were brought before the LORD

against the inhabitants of the land. It therefore concluded that the land mourns and the inhabitants (**all who live in it**) began to waste away. It did not state that the culprits were the casualties alone; rather it's everyone that lives there. The world and its foundation is out of its place, the world system will soon collapse.

Psalm 82:5 (KJV)
²⁵They know not, neither will they understand; they walk on in darkness: All the foundations of the earth are out of course.

Remember, that (Deut. 7:1-2) it is the LORD who will cast out the nations before them. In the ensuing encounter, the people were not waiting and sitting in a cruise station expecting GOD to move ahead, fight the enemy, win the battle and then come back to ferry them on specially designed boats and trains to those promised lands. As a young untrained feeble nation, GOD fought and demonstrated His ever conquering might through the weak.

The Battle is Mostly Spiritual Warfare
In this prophetic agenda, to take over the mountains of Media, Economy, Sports and Entertainment, Family, Politics, Religion and Education; which these mountains represent, we should see them as primarily a contest, battle or warfare. These battles, as we know, though not physical but spiritual warfare must not only be fought but must be seen to be won. We should see these mountains as the LORD sees them. There are occupying our inheritances. They must be deposed and their mountains be repossessed by the covenanted due occupants.

2 Corinthians 10:4-6 (RSV)
⁴for the weapons of our warfare are not worldly but have divine power to destroy strongholds. ⁵We destroy arguments and every proud obstacle to the knowledge of God, and take every thought captive to obey Christ, 6being ready to punish

every disobedience, when your obedience is complete.

The Strategic Level Warfare

In this mountain, we must apply all strategic spiritual weapons of warfare from the arsenal of heaven to depose the enemies of the LORD from these mountains. There are strongholds of mentalities and believe systems we have imbibed for years. The separation of spirituality from secularity has to be debunked and obliterated in this generation and the subsequent ones. We must see the earth as '*the LORD's and fullness thereof*' (Psalm 24:1). All these mountains of influence are part of the fullness thereof. GOD declared that cattles on a thousand hills or mountains belongs to the Him (Ps. 50:10).

We must see the earth as being controlled first of all as a spiritual entity. It is said that the spiritual that governs the physical. Whatever that takes place in the spiritual do manifest in the physically. The scripture says the 'To be worldly minded is death.' Actually, this is a dying world.
Romans 8:6 (KJV)
⁶For to be carnally minded is death; but to be spiritually minded is life and peace.

Gen 1:1: *In the beginning God created the heavens and the earth*. That means that from the inception, GOD had already created all things but will be made manifest from the enabling verses of the book of the beginning. It does mean that the earth was in existence before the creation. JESUS was in existence with the FATHER before HIS manifestation. *In the beginning was the word, the word was with GOD and word was GOD* (John 1:1). He was also killed and his blood shed before the foundation of the earth but was made manifest in our generation in order to redeem us from all negative mindsets.
The Redeemed of the LORD Will Be Qualified

1 Peter 1:18-21 (NKJV) *[18]knowing that you were not redeemed with corruptible things,… [19]but (were redeemed) with the precious blood of Christ, as of a lamb without blemish and without spot. 20He indeed was foreordained before the foundation of the world, but was manifest in these last times for you 21who through Him believe in God, who raised Him glory, so that your faith and hope are in God.*

The redemption which CHRIST purchased for us was not done by silver nor gold which do get corrupt. It redeemed us from certain negative things which were hereditarily being transferred from one generation to another. But the redemption was determined before the foundation of the world.

In the under mentioned scripture, the determining factor is to be strong in the LORD and in the power of His might. But to be enveloped by His defense mechanisms means being assured of the full armor of GOD's protection. In the fullness of His armories is to be guarded and guided in our fullness by His attributes to us. Of all the weapons of our warfare, it is only the word of GOD that is the only offensive weapon.

The Full Armor of Our Warfare
Ephesians 6:10-18 (NIV) - *[10] Finally, be strong in the Lord and in his mighty power. [11]Put on the full armor of God so that you can take your stand against the devil's schemes. [12]For our struggle is not against flesh and blood, but against the rulers, against the authorities, against the powers of this dark world and against the spiritual forces of evil in the heavenly realms. [13]Therefore put on the full armor of God, so that when the day of evil comes, you may be able to stand your ground, and after you have done everything, to stand. [14]Stand firm then, with the belt of truth buckled around your waist, with the breastplate of righteousness in place, [15]and with your feet fitted with the readiness that comes from the gospel of peace. [16]In addition*

to all this, take up the shield of faith, with which you can extinguish all the flaming arrows of the evil one. ¹⁷Take the helmet of salvation and the sword of the Spirit, which is the word of God. ¹⁸And pray in the Spirit on all occasions with all kinds of prayers and requests. With this in mind, be alert and always keep on praying for all the saints.

In the next chapters, we will consider the advancement of the kingdom of GOD through spiritual warfare.

Prayer Points

• LORD JESUS, please show me the controlling principality on each of the seven mountains.

• Give me the strategy to contend with them in battles.

• Give me the proper weapon for each battle in order to be victorious.

• Gird me with the proper armor of warfare.

• Help me LORD to be spiritually minded in everything.

• Make me an eligible kingdom soldier.

ALL these I pray in JESUS name!

Chapter Three

THE NEGLECTED CONFLICT

The Battle is Real

In the organization that I belonged, we defined spiritual warfare as a "combat between the kingdom of darkness and the kingdom of LIGHT." To understand this religious world, globally, I will classify them into two kingdoms. The kingdom of light (GOD) represented by the Church. The kingdom of darkness as represented by the rest of the world religions which has Lucifer as its lord. Interestingly, almost all the world religions are enemies of the Church and Israel either in overt or covert actions.

The most virulent of all religions of the world is Islam. They understand this world and her affairs as a battle which must be won by the Islamists. Unfortunately, the western world is at ease or asleep while the lion is on the prowl at night feigning to be asleep in the day time. No one seemed to be bothered while the protagonists are busy drawing a clandestine Islamic global agenda.

Islam grants radical Muslims a mandate. It is a mandate to change the existing society into an Islamic society. This isn't about building a few mosques for the needs of Muslim congregations, or schools, or a few cultural centers. It is to make Islam supreme, and thus dominate every aspect of society or the seven mountains. This is not only the desire of fundamentalists like, Osama Bin Laden, but from their teaching, preaching and publications, would seem to be the desire of a large number of Muslims all over the world.

In a proper Islamic movement, their ideologies are clearly emphasized on these four elements:
1.   Total Takeover,
2.   The Supremacy of Islam,
3.   Organized Struggle
4.   The Socio-political Dominion and
5.   Economic Empowerment

Total Takeover
        Muslims and their proponents have a global agenda. Nigeria is a case study and battle ground of their experiments. If Moslems could take over a nation by such agenda, Nigeria could have been an Islamic country long ago. This nation called Nigeria had seen more devastation than any other nation in the recent times. Nigeria lost more Christians in 2013 through this Islamic agenda than any nation else. More churches were bombed and people were killed than any other (www.globalislamicagenda.com).
        By going through the annals of history, it could be understood that this was the execution of the so called Abuja conference of Organization of Islamic Countries (OIC) of November 29, 1989. It was agreed by resolution that a total takeover of Nigeria means the takeover of other vassal nations in Africa. This agenda was sponsored by these organizations. It has the following as the core value:
        "To promote Islamic solidarity among member States; to coordinate efforts for the safeguard of the holy places and support of the struggle of the people of Palestine and help them to regain their rights and

32

liberate their land; To strengthen the struggle of all Moslem people with a view to safeguarding their dignity, independence and national rights."

Islamic Global Agenda

Many revelations and reports from within and outside Nigeria have been received. There was and there is a clandestine agenda to Islamize some countries. The agenda is strong, to Islamize the largest black nation is their number one strategy. Their agenda is the same from Cape Town to Cairo. They are usually adamant in the pursuit of their goals. There is large scale awareness in recent times of the schemes of Islamic proponents. It was made worst during the military regimes of the cabals from the northern part of Nigeria.

There was certain classified information that filtered into the ears of the Nigerian Churches. *There were many fears about the unity of the nation called Nigeria. The public fears were further fueled by a letter from the Christian Council of South Africa, addressed to the Elders-in-Charge of the churches and Christian missions in Nigeria, written in October 1988. The letter warned of the imminent plan to disrupt Nigeria.*

It revealed the: "Proposed plot by northern Moslems and their Arab OIC supporters to destroy churches, carry out mass murder of Christians in Nigeria (with more intensity in the Northern States of Nigeria); Counterplot by the South African Defense Forces to launch an offensive on Nigeria to defeat the Arabs and their OIC-backed Northern Nigerian Moslems" (Dr. Femi Ajayi, Public Relation Consultants, Atlanta-Georgia).

All coup d'états and counter coups are the Islamic agenda to regulate the political destiny of this great nation Nigeria. The Federal Government of Nigeria's Helsmanship of a Moslem in the 1980s and their special donations to the Islamic Development Fund of the OIC for the total Islamization of Nigeria in particular and Africa in general has always been a prove of such agenda.

*To confirm the assertion, the '***Islam in Africa Organization***' held a conference in Abuja on November 28, 1989, and resolved among other things: "To ensure the ultimate replacement of all western forms of legal and judicial systems with the Sharia in all member nations before the next Islam in Africa Conference. The conference notes the yearnings of Muslims everywhere on the continent who have been deprived of their rights to be governed by the Sharia and urges them to intensify efforts in the struggle to reinstate the application of the Sharia"* (**Dr. Femi Ajayi**).

But in Christianity, it seemed to be the worst in terms of the above mentioned ideological elements. To crown it all, Christianity has little or no ideology. We were taught in the Church that politics is corrupt and should not be attempted by a heavenly bound member. In Islam, it is the opposite.

Consider the account of the Uthman Dan Fodio led jihad of the pre-colonial period of Nigeria. The Muslim enclave of Northern Nigeria was fought and defeated by the invaders from the Arab nations. The region of the Northern people of the then Nigeria was not spared of the war even when it was an Islamic enclave already. Dan Fodio said, '**to seize power is obligatory by accent**'. Therefore to purify the religion of its accretion and syncretism is not less important as to seize power.

The Hope of Nigeria is Church

The Church in Nigeria is a praying Church. I may be tempted to state that the level of prayers that ascends to GOD from Nigeria is greater than any other country in the world. The sayings that the 'night is usually ticker at the breaking of the day'; is real. There is hope for nations that prays.

Islam established their religion on falsehood and propaganda. Most of their population statistics are doctored in many Christian dominated enclaves of Africa.

Population Propaganda

Just imagine the statement of Ahmadu Bello the first compromised premier in Nigeria. *The nation called Nigeria should be an estate of our great grandfathers, Uthman Dan Fodio. We must ruthlessly prevent a change of power. We will use the minorities in the North as willing tools and the South as conquered territory and never allow them to rule over us and never allow them to have control of their future. - Sir Ahmadu Bello.* First published by Parrot October 12, 1960 and made public by Tribune of Nov 13, 2002.

Population Propaganda

He acknowledged that the Northern Nigeria is in minority. How come that the population of Nigeria in 1963 is 70% Muslims? Why were the Muslims in Nigeria insisting that the column for the religion must be removed in 2006 population census? That falsehood must be obliterated. In Nigeria, Muslim population is 30% while the Christian population is 60% other animist religion shares 10%.

Their mission and vision is constant. These are three most profound instruments in spreading and propagating Islam worldwide. They are: Economic and Population evangelism in addition to terrorism as her military strategy. We cannot comprehend the mountain of family until we consider the impact of Islam and her strategy to entrench her religion through this mountain of family.

Their conspiracy of one man four wives and a minimum of four children per wife is one of the strongest tools in using insurrection through population advantage to establish Islam.

While the western nations are busy propounding birth control and legitimizing gay marriages, the nations of Islam are promoting polygamy while population expansionism as veritable tool.

The end result is that the population of the West is doomed to stagnate as nations are forced to legitimize same sex marriages and legalize abortions with impunity. The Islamic nations are busy exporting their youth to the West en mass. This will definitely spell doom in the next two decades. Before the Western nations will wake up from their slumber it will be very late indeed.

Their strategy is long-term, well focused and constantly pursued. In a country of absolute Muslim minority; they work hard to increase their population within a stipulated period. They do this, by exporting their youth en mass as peasant workers with a charge to multiply and increase there. They will act as spies to the Muslim rich men by informing them of potential business opportunities. When the rich eventually arrives, they will use the peasants to start a mosque. Gradually, they will be empowered financially. The next agenda will be to marry four wives and raise multiple children. When their population appreciates, they will network with the media houses to increase their voices as a pressure group.

Some African countries are being intimidated and pressured by the West to legitimize gay marriages or face suspension of their so-called economic aids. Nothing is said of Islamic nations that has made homosexual act-a-capital offence. The intolerable nature of the Muslims of any form of criticism of their piety is a weapon for their undue freedom and expansion project.

A recent survey had shown that in France the Muslim population will be in majority in the next 25 years.

The recent protest from the Muslim youths in France against the ban on public wearing of veils was a litmus test that the nation is progressing towards unprecedented Muslim domination. It is noteworthy that a 10% of Muslim population in any non-Muslim nation is a great asset to the religion. With this mere percentage, aggressive drive to be heard, noticed and recognized becomes inevitable.

Nations are at ease with a deadly religious virus. The venom of the West against Christianity is a conspiracy of the Illuminati and her network of global cultism to resist and if possible expunge the very foundation of eternal order of life is a warfare strategy. To tolerate Islam in the West and prosecute wars against the Church is to accept to live in the forest with predator than at home with pets.

The Islamic global agenda is real. Its advancement is aggressively pursued but helplessly ignored. One day the Western nations will wake up with the blast of their Al Akbar in their streets and it will be too late.

In the view of the last protest against the public wearing of veil in France, there were mass scale reactions from across the Muslim world. The protesters also say that *"our eyes are on Paris, our eyes are on Brussels, and our eyes are on London. We will not stop, as Muslims, until the whole world is governed by Islam."*

Islam's proponents are not in a hurry. Their agenda is a long-term agenda. They have the time and strategy being globally funded by Petro Dollars.

The growth of this religious sect is proven to be the fastest in United States. The youths are highly attracted to the same religion that has given them more sorrows than ever. The Church is busy eroding into apostasy. Prayers have been neglected and lost in the Church and in families.

How do they intend to achieve it? They said, *"Put the seeds down for an Islamic Emirate in the long term"*. This is very simple to understand. We will not keep quite in this our generation. We need to heed the call of Mordecai to Esther.

Esther 4:14 (NIV)

[14] *"For if you remain silent at this time, relief and deliverance for the Jews will arise from another place, but you and your father's family will perish. And who knows but that you have come to royal position for such a time as this?"*

We will not keep quite in the face of this advancing asteroid. We cannot deploy physical weapon, we will deploy heavenly weapons of warfare. Our prayers are more than enough. The way the communist advancement collapsed is the way Islam will crumble.

Prayer Points

•   Ask GOD to cause a large scale global awareness on of all the schemes of the Muslims all over the nations

•   Ask the LORD to reveal to the Western nations the soon coming doom if they keep silent on Islamic advancement

•   Command that their global agenda will be frustrated

•   Pray that their global terrorist network be paralyzed completely

•   That GOD will frustrate their counsels

•   That GOD will encounter, arrest and convert strong Islamic clerics and use them to destroy Islam

•   Declare that this the time of judgment on Islam.

- Pray that GOD will raise men of GOD that will pass judgments on Islam

Chapter Four

THRESHING PROCESS

The Class of Army That GOD Will Not Use

Who are those inhabiting the mountains and how can we contend with them in battles? These are the giants of all the unconquered territories. They are champions or warriors from their youths (1 Sam. 17:33). GOD promised to transform the weakest vessel to a new but threshing instrument. GOD likened the weak vessel as worm. Can worm fight? GOD promised that He will help worm Israel and transform her as great weapon that will subdue the mountains.

Isaiah 41:14-17(NIV)

[14]Do not be afraid, O worm Jacob, O little Israel, for I myself will help you," declares the Lord your Redeemer, the Holy One of Israel.
[15]"See, I will make you into a threshing sledge, new and sharp, with many teeth. You will thresh the mountains and crush them, and reduce the hills to chaff. [16]You will winnow them, the wind will pick them up, and a gale will blow them away. But you will rejoice in the Lord and glory in the Holy One of Israel. [17]The poor and needy search for water, but there is none; their tongues are parched with thirst. But I the Lord will answer them; I, the God of Israel, will not forsake them.

Threshing process is needed in order to select the wanted items and discard the unwanted ones. Can GOD use a weakling boneless worm to do anything good?

The elder brothers of David rebuked him for being inquisitive in a professional warfare rather than his dedicated duty as an overseer of a few flock in the field. They never knew that he was the man to win. Having been running from Goliath for about forty years, yet they had no clue that the savior has emerged. Such army and its leadership will not be used by GOD

1 Samuel 17:3-7 (NIV)
³The Philistines occupied one hill and the Israelites another, with the valley between them.
⁴A champion named Goliath, who was from Gath, came out of the Philistine camp. He was over nine feet tall. ⁵He had a bronze helmet on his head and wore a coat of scale armor of bronze weighing five thousand shekels; ⁶ on his legs he wore bronze greaves, and a bronze javelin was slung on his back. ⁷His spear shaft was like a weaver's rod, and its iron point weighed six hundred shekels. His shield bearer went ahead of him.

Which type of hill were the Israelites occupying? The Philistines were also on the opposing hill. If we consider their intimidating record of victories in warfare, we could tarry too long on this mountain or rather be defeated. The emerging David was a youthful soldier with proportionate curriculum vitae. He was burdened and troubled by the insult to the armies of the Living GOD. He came like a woman in the delivery room travailing to bring forth her child.

We need to develop such similar burden for this world that's full of apostasy, hypocrisy, blasphemy and reprobacy towards GOD. We are in the era of religious syncretism. We are compromising our pure biblical worships and obligations with the worldly negative social considerations.

Moses refused to be called the son of Pharaoh's daughter (Heb. 11:24) when it was revealed to him of his ancestry. Daniel purposed in his hearth that he will not defile himself with the king's idolatrous delicacies (Dan. 1:8). May such mindset, attitude and attribute be found in you in JESUS name!

We are in the last days, we must keep to our mind that there will be stubborn resistance on all the mountains in the promised lands.

Joshua 17:12-13 (NIV)
12 Yet the Manassites were not able to occupy these towns, for the Canaanites were determined to live in that region. 13 However, when the Israelites grew stronger, they subjected the Canaanites to forced labor but did not drive them out completely.

GOD forbid that we shall act like the Manassites and or Ephraimites, respectively, as in the under mentioned scripture. Consequently, the tribe of Manasseh were sore afraid and gave occasion for the resistance of the Canaanites. Even with their resistance and determination not to be displaced, Israel grew stronger and subjected them. But, that was not good enough, they were not removed entirely. Subsequently, they rather grew and started incessant insurrections.

Psalms 78:9-10 (NKJV)
9 The children of Ephraim, being armed and carrying bows, Turned back in the day of battle. 10 They did not keep the covenant of God; They refused to walk in His law,

Also, these Ephraimite soldiers cannot be the type of the armies of the LORD that will put to flight all the enemy soldiers on our mountains. The description was that there were armed with sophisticated weapons, perhaps well trained in tactical warfare but were defeated by intimidation and fear. They turned back in the day of battle. That was a fatal blow to such a kingdom that has such an army. May we not run in the day of battle! Ephraimites ran away in the day of decision.

In another development in the scriptures, there was a place known as Gibeath-elohim, Gibeah of GOD or hill of GOD in many biblical translations. When Saul was anointed, as part of his commissioning and confirmation by the prophet; he was given divine prophetic directions. Part of which was the gift of prophecy. Consider the following transaction:

1 Samuel 10:5-7 (NIV)
[5]"After that you will go to Gibeah of God, where there is a Philistine outpost. As you approach the town, you will meet a procession of prophets coming down from the high place with lyres, tambourines, flutes and harps being played before them, and they will be prophesying. [6]The Spirit of the LORD will come upon you in power, and you will prophesy with them; and you will be changed into a different person. [7]Once these signs are fulfilled, do whatever your hand finds to do, for God is with you.

How can a king who was anointed, commissioned and baptized with the Holy Ghost be so unperturbed with the Hill of GOD being occupied by the philistine armed forces? They were not only there but, have established effective occupation by building their command post on the mountain dedicated to and called by the name of GOD.

It could be according to the suggestion of the following text: *Rather, after they were subdued in the beginning of his time they got ground again, so far as to force this garrison into that place, and thence God raised up the man that should chastise them. There was a place that was called the hill of God, because of one of the schools of the prophets built upon it; and such respect did even Philistines themselves pay to religion that a garrison of their soldiers* *suffered a school of God's prophets to live peaceably by them, and did not only not dislodge them, but not restrain nor disturb the public exercises of their devotion (**Source: Matthew Henry's Commentary on the Whole Bible, ©2006 by Biblesoft, Inc**.).*

GOD cannot raise these types of army. They were physically   qualified but spiritually not. In the former two case studies, they were trained and commissioned but were fainthearted indeed. They were faithless. GOD wants those that can move by faith and not by sight. The later was spiritually commissioned but has no faith in his ability at that time.

The report of the ten spies of Moses and the multitude was another case study. Joshua and Caleb were seeing possibilities the rest saw giants, and lands that swallows its inhabitant. They even described themselves as grasshoppers before the giants. That was grasshopper mentality.

Such bands were as the four hundred prophets, who were inquired of by King Ahab in company of King Jehoshaphat of Judah.

1 Kings 22:6-7 (NIV)
⁶So the king of Israel brought together the prophets — about four hundred men — and asked them, "Shall I go to war against Ramoth Gilead, or shall I refrain?"

The prophets began to prophesy, they told him what he would ever want to hear. But Jehoshaphat discerned them as counterfeit. And he asked his friend, *⁷"…Is there not a prophet of the LORD here whom we can inquire of?"*

Jehoshaphat asked a simple question. Is there not 'a' prophet to inquire of? We don't actually need bands of prophets. To have a whole lot of four hundred sons of the prophets prophesying in a synagogue or in the palace is a great noise. We need just one man of GOD with the word of GOD. He (Prophet Micaiah) was described by one man of GOD as prophet number 401. He distinguished his message from the lot of the multitudes. His number was four hundred and one after the noisy lot. The lists of such that must be threshed from the LORD's army are inexhaustive.

My mentor use to describe certain churches as having the mentality of 'always bless syndrome'. He analyzed our Lord's Prayer in this way:
1.   Our father who is in heaven
2.   Hallowed be your name
3.   May your kingdom come
4.   May your will be done on earth as in heaven
5.   Give us this day and our daily bread---.

In this sequence, our personal prayers for our personal blessings should come as the fifth point. The armies of these days are interested in their own kingdom being established rather than the kingdom of GOD.

Another tragedy is the regime of Samson. The bible described it as such, **Judges 15:20 (NLT)**
[20]Samson judged Israel for twenty years during the period when the Philistines dominated the land.

What kind of ruler is Governor Samson? He was like a Ruler, a Pastor or President in his domain for twenty years but the heathen were in charge of the resources of the land. This is no doubt the state of the church of today. We lead large congregation but the people of the world are in charge of the resources of the land. They control every business and all we can always do is to write 'I humbly apply' to serve them.

JESUS made a hearth throbbing lamentation in

Luke 16:8: *...for the children of this world are in their generation wiser than the children of light.* (KJV)

How can we become the conquering army of the LORD? Who will lead us to the mountains? Certainly, not the army that is plagued by sins, compromise, immorality, faithlessness, infidelity and racial or ethnic recrimination.

We mourn the destiny of businesses in certain parts of developing countries especially in Africa. Businesses don't get transferred to the next generation. Also in the church, some big churches, ministries and businesses of Christian brethren don't exceed the lifespan of the founders. There is always a generational gap. How do we bridge the gap?

As owners of mega and medium sized corporations in developed countries are busy raising great oaks in their families to succeed them. As certain family owned businesses are busy preparing their offspring for generational transition; as owners of mega corporations are training potential leaders to take the organizations to greater heights. We see a lot of generational gaps in the church. We are not building to last, such Chief Executive Officers (CEOs) cannot be enlisted in the coming divine selection process.

The lack of trained human resources is the major cause of leadership woes and generational gaps. Who will learn from each other, the church or the world? The industrial revolution was sparked off through the church. An untrained army is a security risk in any nation. We need a people prepared for the soon coming revolution. For it is said that everything rises and falls upon leadership.

The greatest tragedy of the black race is a monster called tribalism. It comes in different apparels as ethnicity, nepotism and favoritism

Prayer Points

46

- Declare that you will not see impossibilities but possibilities.

- Ask GOD to baptize you with unconditional faith.

- Ask GOD to thresh the present fearful army and select a Davidic army.

- Ask GOD to help you as a worm and transform you as a threshing instrument.

- Proclaim that you will not be like the Manassite or Ephraimite soldiers who turn back on the day of battle.

- As GOD to give you His word as He gave to prophet Micaiah to be distinguished from common bands of prophets.

- Ask GOD to train you in this coming revelation to be enlisted as those that will possess the mountains.

Chapter Five

THE SELECTION PROCESS

In this emerging army of the LORD there will be selection. GOD will set apart those that are eligibly qualified and that, by Himself. He will separate the weak from the strong, righteous from the unrighteous. He will use both feeble and mighty men at different times and seasons and in different situations and circumstances as the occasion demands.

The word selection means to set apart, consecrate or commission for a special purpose. In several portions of the scripture; GOD commanded that certain men be set apart for special assignments. The tribe of Levi was set apart for ministerial assignment.

Dimensions of Setting Apart

There are those that are known to be set apart, separated, consecrated or commissioned by the LORD in His divine prerogative. This class of people will never have an alternative. The election will fall upon them from birth. Samson was a typical example. He became ordained even before he was conceived.

Judges 13:5 (NIV)
⁵...No razor may be used on his head, because the boy is to be a Nazirite, set apart to God from birth, and he will begin the deliverance of Israel from the hands of the Philistines."

Another great personality which the LORD selected in such a manner was Prophet Jeremiah. His selection was communicated to him directly as a youth.

Jeremiah 1:5 (NIV)

⁵ "Before I formed you in the womb I knew you, before you were born I set you apart; I appointed you as a prophet to the nations."

Apostle Paul was a mystery among these similar circumstances. He was a tent maker and never stopped making tents throughout his life. He was called; no doubt, but answered the call wrongly in the same passion but in an opposing camp. There are many of such men who are called in same reminiscent manner; but there are still in a certain secular business so to say, either in one ministerial business, fulfilling one ministry calling or in a wrong and false religious ministry. GOD will locate them as He did with Paul.

Galatians 1:15-17 (NLT)

¹⁵ But even before I was born, God chose me and called me by his marvelous grace. Then it pleased him ¹⁶to reveal his Son to me so that I would proclaim the Good News about Jesus to the Gentiles. When this happened, I did not rush out to consult with any human being. ¹⁷Nor did I go up to Jerusalem to consult with those who were apostles before I was. Instead, I went away into Arabia, and later I returned to the city of Damascus.

Conversely, there are certain tribes or a people from one geographical location whom GOD has endowed with a redemptive gift as he did with the tribe of Levi. My prayer to them is that GOD will graciously set them apart in this dispensation for His eternal purposes.

Amos 7:14-15 (KJV)
[14]Then answered Amos, and said to Amaziah, I was no prophet, neither was I a prophet's son; but I was an herdman, and a gatherer of sycomore fruit: [15]And the Lord took me as I followed the flock, and the Lord said unto me, Go, prophesy unto my people Israel.

Men and women in the reminiscent manner of Amos will be elected by divine mandate. Their ministries are mostly unusual. They are peculiar in nature. They may not have the right approach or formal training to function. But, GOD usually allows them to carry heavier mandate in order to confound the wise through them. In this our peculiar dispensation, GOD will call many into some peculiar assignments. It may require that such could relinquish the profession momentarily but will return to the same profession afterwards. It may bring about a great a revolution in the society SMEs.

Deuteronomy 10:8 (NIV)
[8]At that time the LORD set apart the tribe of Levi to carry the ark of the covenant of the LORD, to stand before the LORD to minister and to pronounce blessings in his name, as they still do today.

The last set of people that will fall into the next selection processes are those who will not be naturally eligible, but they will be raised to replace those who are called but refuse to align themselves to the eternal mandate. Others are those who will, by their zeal and sacrifice break forth into an enviable apogee in certain field of endeavor that will endear them to the Master.

Numbers 25:11-13 (NIV)
[11]"Phinehas son of Eleazar, the son of Aaron, the priest, has turned my anger away from the Israelites; for he was as zealous as I am for my honor among them, so that in my zeal I

did not put an end to them. [12]"Therefore tell him I am making my covenant of peace with him. [13]He and his descendants will have a covenant of a lasting priesthood, because he was zealous for the honor of his God and made atonement for the Israelites."

A peculiar instruction of divine selection was recorded in Acts of the Apostle when, by divine prerogative, the Holy Spirit commanded that certain apostles should be set apart for a special assignment. Note that there were worshipping the LORD when the instruction came.

Acts 13:2-3 (NIV)
[2]While they were worshiping the Lord and fasting, the Holy Spirit said, "Set apart for me Barnabas and Saul for the work to which I have called them." [3]So after they had fasted and prayed, they placed their hands on them and sent them off.

There are certain people that will be called and set apart for a peculiar ministry while they might be doing great exploits for GOD in the church. I love to be in the Church services, but sometimes, I could be moved for a special assignment for a season. In this season of abundance of grace there are going to be selection of eligible, ineligible and unqualified people by our standards.

In almost all the instances given above, one particular transaction was pertinent. The commissioning process was necessary. David and Saul were commissioned by the same hand, the same oil from one horn and by the same prophet. Without being anointed by the prophet, Saul and David would have ended their careers as shepherds of family cattle. Oftentimes, GOD may anoint them divinely on His own as in the circumstances with Samson and Jeremiah. But we need anointing to excel in all our endeavors.

I recommend Jonny Enlow's book on Seven Mountain Prophecies to you. He talked about Elijah's revolution. A sweeping -Tsunami type of revolution that will overthrow the kingdoms represented as the Mountains. I began to reminisce about Elijah's revolution. The Spirit of the LORD quickened me to an understanding. Elijah's revolution was not an enduring revolution. Elijah had neither an army nor well trained disciples who were prepared to midwife the revolution he birthed. He did a spontaneous act and ran away. He couldn't call down any more fire at the threat of Jezebel. He disappointed GOD.

GOD has never encouraged fear in any part of the scripture. Fear is the opposite of faith. Rather, in the entire book of the bible there are about three hundred and sixty 'Fear not'. That means that daily, there is a word to us saying, 'fear not'. Therefore, any day we exhibit fear, it's like a vote of no confidence to the His promises. Fear and faithlessness is a great sin before the LORD. It should be seen as act of sabotage to our great GOD. The scripture made a clear definition of GOD's stand on the issue of not having faith in Hebrews 11:6.

Hebrews 11:6
6And without faith it is impossible to please God, because anyone who comes to him must believe that he exists and that he rewards those who earnestly seek him.

GOD is in the business of looking for those who will trust him unconditionally. Jonathan was the kind of man GOD desires to raise in our generation (1Sam. 13). Those who can move towards the mountains of the Amorites by faith, he alone put to flight a whole regiment without a back-up from anywhere.

I was given a topic by my local church to develop in our bible study outline. The topic was on faith. I posted this description, 'Faith is unconditional trust unto GOD without plan B'. If anyone has plan B in his trust with GOD it has ceased to be faith.

Gideon came to the bank of the river with thirty two thousand soldiers. The LORD declared:

Judges 7:3 (NKJV)
³'Whoever is fearful and afraid, let him turn and depart at once from Mount Gilead.'" And twenty-two thousands of the people returned, and ten thousand remained.

Yet, GOD was still determined to show himself strong; He went further by reducing the numbers as thus:

Judges 7:5-6 (NIV)
⁵"Separate those who lap the water with their tongues like a dog from those who kneel down to drink." ⁶Three hundred men lapped with their hands to their mouths. All the rest got down on their knees to drink.

These were how He raised and trained the men through Gideon. GOD is the sole power that can determine our eligibilities and qualifications. He proved here that it is not by power nor by might but by His Spirit. GOD declared that the battle is not ours but His. All we need to do is stand still in an unwavering and unconditional trust on Him. Then we will see His salvation.

Luke 6:12-14 (NIV)
¹²One of those days Jesus went out to a mountainside to pray, and spent the night praying to God. ¹³When morning came, he called his disciples to him and chose twelve of them, whom he also designated apostles: ¹⁴Simon (whom he named Peter), his brother Andrew, James, John, Philip, Bartholomew,

JESUS prayed all night, called, chose and designated them. GOD needs people who are called, chosen and designated to be an army for His kingdom.

David welcomed the four hundred men. Every one of them has a pronounced social reproach.

1 Samuel 22:2 (NIV) - *²All those who were in distress or in*

53

debt or discontented gathered around him, and he became their leader. About four hundred men were with him.

David's disposition in both accepting and training these destitute was a great lesson for leaders and would be leaders. Consider their contributions in the nation's armed forces. They exhibited the greatest feat in history. They never lost any battle. May GOD give us men to discover, train and equip in order to get the best out of them.

Joshua mobilized an army. The same people who were intimidated in the wilderness of Kadesh at Shittim by death, a people battered by immoralities with the Midianitish women, a people defeated by fear of the giants, a people of massive unbelief, a people of great fear and murmuring and of all negative characteristics. When they got united and decided to march forward, the heavens reacted with approvals. When the LORD saw these acts, that they had risen to march forward as soldiers, He sent the universal military commander from above. To lead a people prepared for the LORD's bidding.

Joshua 5:13-15 (NIV)
[13]Now when Joshua was near Jericho, he looked up and saw a man standing in front of him with a drawn sword in his hand. Joshua went up to him and asked, "Are you or us or for our enemies?" [14]"Neither," he replied, "but as commander of the army of the Lord I have now come." Then Joshua fell facedown to the ground in reverence, and asked him, "What message does my Lord d have for his servant?" [15]The commander of the Lord's army replied, "Take off your sandals, for the place where you are standing is holy." And Joshua did so.

GOD is still awaiting a people that are united and are ready to go forward.

Luke 1:17 (NIV)
…To make ready a people prepared for the Lord."

I've known, seen and even ministered in several

meetings of certain group of peculiar people. Such groups that are called: Apostles in the market place, the Tent Makers International, Kingdom professional's fellowship, Fellowship of one Christian body or the order in one organization or another. All these are indications that the LORD is really raising people to possess the mountains of influences.

Prayer Points

- Ask GOD to set you apart and make you a peculiar person in your calling and work with him.

- Pray for definite encounter(s) that will transform and change your mind set and attitude.

- Tell GOD earnestly to confirm your present calling in order to know if you are in the right place of service.

- Pray that you will always be relevant and to fulfill your calling effectively.

- Ask GOD to deliver you from any negative or sin habit that may hinder you from possessing your mountain.

Chapter Six

REMNANT GENERATION

Our GOD is continually advancing His mandate towards the remnant generation as He promised. A remnant is a residue of a people who remains loyal and faithful to a vision whenever the people or nation goes astray. Throughout the whole Bible, the people of GOD and nations at large have always had a remnant which, GOD preserves to return back to Him and restore order to the subsequent generations. Consider the under mentioned scriptures. It shows that the zeal of the LORD of hosts will drive the establishment of the remnants from the Church.

Ninety percent of men of influence with GOD are usually men that are despised, neglected and dubbed as never important. When those who are born great are being trained and prepared for greatness, a true remnant will manifest from obscurity and take over from the potential successors. Remnants are peculiar in nature, virtually unknown, and properly out of position. They are usually the one that will be established afterwards.

2 Kings 19:30-31 (NIV)
30Once more a remnant of the house of Judah will take root below and bear fruit above. 31 For out of Jerusalem will come a remnant, and out of mount Zion a band of survivors. The zeal

56

of the Lord Almighty will accomplish this.

There is Always a Remnant Generation

Once more indicates that it has happened before and will happen again. The import of the phrase; **'to take root beneath bear fruit above'** means that they (the remnants) will be established as a tree planted by the side of a river. Their roots shall be shored upon the earth and will bear fruit above. Besides that, only the zeal of the LORD will accomplish that.

This remnant company is everywhere and in every generation. There are upon all the mountains. In this generation of moral decadence; where every word of GOD is weighed on the balance of social considerations and found wanting. There are still those who are mourning and crying for the restoration of true kingdom values and virtues (Ezek. 9:4-6). Before the destruction of any nation or a system, GOD will strategically make provisions for the preservation of the remnants.

These are the responsibilities of the remnants:

- Those that will be spared after a great destruction in a nation or a system.

- Those that will be kept to suffer the aftermath of the misdeeds of their generation or the system.

- Those that will give the accounts of the demise of the people.

- Those that will replenish the nation or the system.

- Those that will start the rebuilding and restoration process.

57

- Those who will instruct the successive generations to keep and maintain order.

I perceive strongly in my spirit that there will be a great shaking in the global market places (in the seven mountains) such that has never been and will never be again. The coming shaking will make the era of former global recession and recent global meltdown to look like a child's play. GOD will orchestrate such global catastrophe to hit the world atheistic systems that hold sway on the seven mountains. In this soon coming shakings, the LORD himself has prepared a remnant generation.

A Remnant Must be Spared
Isaiah 10:22 (TLB)
²² But though Israel be now as many as the sands along the shore, yet only a few of them will be left to return at that time; God has rightly decided to destroy his people.

This scripture is very critical. GOD has decreed a coming great and unprecedented destruction. But only a remnant shall be spared. These remnants are the ones that will bring an enduring transformation. They will establish the counsel of GOD in the global marketplaces. They will be the company to emerge for the eventual wealth transfer and total takeover of the seven mountains.

At that time, the words of GOD spoken by Nebuchadnezzar of erstwhile Babylonian empire will witness against this generation.

Daniel 4:17 (NIV)
¹⁷ " 'The decision is announced by messengers, the holy ones declare the verdict, so that the living may know that the Most High is sovereign over the kingdoms of men and gives them to anyone he wishes and sets over them the lowliest of men.'

Nebuchadnezzar had built a nation and an empire without GOD.   He glorified his capabilities for the hanging gardens; one of the world's wonders of its time.

Emergence of a Rebuilder Company

A rebuilder company will emerge from obscurity. This could be called the Obed-Edom company. The Ark of the covenants of Israel was in the house of Abinadab for about three years. He never learnt how to reverence GOD in this altar (the Ark). There was a calamity when Uzzah stretched out his hand to help GOD from falling. The Ark was abandoned. Obed-Edom took and housed the Ark for three months. He and his family reverence the LORD before the Ark (1 Sam. 6:6-11).

2 Samuel 6:11(KJV)
[11]And the Lord blessed Obed-Edom, and all his household.

It may have been impossible for Obed-Edom's name heard or to achieve greatness. He became a faithful remnant. David himself was scared of the Ark for the death of Uzzah the priest. GOD made him a great man and for many generations. The children of Obed Edom were renowned and influential in all their generations.

This particular rebuilder company of a people will rebuild, restore and transform the desolate places. They will be called by their works - the repairer of the broken walls and restorer of dwelling pathways.

Rebuilding the Desolations
Isaiah 58:12 (KJV)
[12] And they that shall be of thee (the remnants) shall build the old waste places: thou shalt raise up the foundations of many generations; and thou shalt be called, The repairer of the breach, The restorer of paths to dwell in.

It doesn't matter how long the desolations had

lasted or how great was the measure of the damages. This company will take absolute responsibilities not only to repair and restore but to see that the restoration is affected. The key words hereunder are: rebuild, restore and renew. Can GOD find a few remnant in our generation who will take these three dimensional processes of transformation?

Isa 61:4 (NIV)
⁴They will rebuild the ancient ruins
and restore the places long devastated;
they will renew the ruined cities
that have been devastated for generations.

The Soon Coming Shaking

After the shakings, GOD will bring Africa, the lowliest of the all the kingdoms of nations and set her on top of the mountains. GOD's prophetic agenda for the nations is presently tilting to Africa. Africa is the place for the next move of GOD in the committee of nations. This is a prophecy from the Spirit of GOD.

The world is presently and gradually moving towards a total global decay and the emergence of a worldly system where GOD is abhorred. The world is fast drifting into an atheistic order which is being fashioned by the New Age Movement known as the New World Order. It is the Church in Africa that has remained and will remain faithful to heavenly agenda. The world is about to be eclipsed into a catastrophe. There is a wave and manifestation of the church without the Living GOD. The Church in Europe and America is about to outlive her usefulness.

The next dispensation is the dispensation of Africa's time of restoration. The rape by the Western Nations on Africa's economy, the degradation of her environments and fragrant violation of environmental and human rights in exploration of minerals, the abuse, aiding and abetting due processes by the super powers and their business cabals.

They will not be spared in the coming shacking.

Though Africa is known as primary producers since the world began, we have a natural GOD's given advantage. Our ecosystem and climate conditions are Africa's veritable advantage in the coming age. In the next few years, Africa will become the food basket of the nations of the world again. In the time of Joseph, Africa was the food basket of all nations. The natural vegetation is our age long heritage. This is the only continent that fertilizers are not needed to breed crops and vegetables.

Prayer Points

- If you are a remnant in your generation, ask GOD to establish your root downwards and cause your shoot to bear fruits above

- Pray that GOD will install determination to succeed in your life

- Enter a covenant of preservation with the LORD. That whatever that may happen, your life will be preserved

- Ask GOD to rearrange and reposition you for greater responsibilities

- Ask for grace to patiently wait for the appointed time of the LORD

- Pray earnestly for a mandate to be rebuilder among the builders

- Ask GOD to give you the master plan of rebuilding the rots on the mountains

Chapter Seven

UNDERSTANDING THE MANDATE

A look at the dictionary meaning of mandate states as follows:

1. **authoritative order:** an official command or instruction from an authority.
2. **support from electorate:** the authority bestowed on a government or other organization by an electoral victory, effectively authorizing it to carry out the policies for which it campaigned (Source: Microsoft Encarta 2009).

The church of GOD has been given the mandate - power and authority to rule as kingdom of priests and kings on the earth. (Rev. 2:6)

It is unfortunate that we have failed to recognize this GOD's given mandate. In Exodus 19:5, GOD's original design was to raise Israel as a kingdom of priests. This mandate was lost at Mount Horeb as a result of Idolatry. Idolatry means raising an alternative system without GOD. But GOD put in motion a strategic agenda by which, the mandate was restored to man in CHRIST JESUS.

Matt 28:18-19 (NIV)
18"All authority in heaven and on earth has been given to me.
19Therefore go and make disciples of all nations…"

      Whatever that is the LORD's is ours. The authority has been given to us the kingdom citizens. Many who recognize this have been doing exploits. But those living in ignorance are still awaiting the authority. The book of Daniel expresses this.

Daniel 11:32b (KJV)
..but the people that do know their God shall be strong, and do exploits.

      Where we are raised is far above the reach of those human negative satanic structures. We need to understand in principle that we are operating from the highest echelon of power, seated and established to rain with the King of kings whose reign is from generation to generation.

Ephesians 2:6 (NIV)
6And God raised us up with Christ and seated us with him in the heavenly realms in Christ Jesus,

      We have been raised up with Christ. Our spiritual position is in heaven, above all the mountains of negative principalities and powers.

Ephesians 3:10-11 (NIV)
10 His intent was that now, through the church, the manifold wisdom of God should be made known to the rulers and authorities (principalities and powers) in the heavenly realms,
11according to his eternal purpose which he accomplished in Christ Jesus our Lord.

      Our LORD's eternal purpose (mandate) which is accomplished in JESUS was, is and will be to use the Church to demonstrate to the world the manifold wisdom of GOD in all the mountains of influence.

In this period of exercising the dominion mandate, many Pharaohs will emerge, in their heart they will want to keep GOD's people and their inheritances into perpetual bondage. They used their slave labors to build their economy (pyramid). They will try to emasculate their male folks and deplete their population. Pharaohs did not know that the time of freedom has come.

Before time of any Jubilee, there are certain responsibilities we will undertake. We will learn how to abide and abase ourselves. How to endure hardship as good soldiers of the LORD is also a compulsory attribute towards manifesting His dominion. We need to obtain grace to deal with the works of the flesh and mortify it. It was afterwards that GOD began to use Moses.

Otherwise, he would have destroyed GOD's inheritance out of anger as he did to the Egyptian (Exo. 2:14).

Exodus 5:1-2 (KJV)
[1] And afterward Moses and Aaron went in, and told Pharaoh, Thus saith the Lord God of Israel, Let my people go, that they may hold a feast unto me in the wilderness.
[2] And Pharaoh said, <u>Who is the Lord, that I should obey his voice to let Israel go? I know not the Lord, neither will I let Israel go</u>.

Pharaoh was very correct, he never knew of any other god save the goddesses in River Nile. How then can one expect him to obey whom he has never heard of or ever know? Even when Moses and Aaron finished the introduction it was a mockery for Pharaoh to surrender to mere men. Then GOD decided to do extraordinary thing; to elevate Moses as GOD unto Pharaoh.

Exodus 7:1-5 (NIV)
[1]Then the Lord said to Moses, "<u>See, I have made you like God</u>

to Pharaoh, and your brother Aaron will be your prophet.
²You are to say everything I command you, and your brother Aaron is to tell Pharaoh to let the Israelites go out of his country. ³But I will harden Pharaoh's heart, and though I multiply my miraculous signs and wonders in Egypt, ⁴he will not listen to you. Then I will lay my hand on Egypt and with mighty acts of judgment I will bring out my divisions, my people the Israelites. ⁵And the Egyptians will know that I am the Lord when I stretch out my hand against Egypt and bring the Israelites out of it."

This is the period of manifesting the power of GOD's kingdom and exercising dominion mandate. GOD will elevate His people to be carriers of his attributes, personality and power.

1 Kings 17:1-2 (NKJV)
¹And Elijah the Tishbite, of the inhabitants of Gilead, said to Ahab, "As the LORD God of Israel lives, before whom I stand, there shall not be dew nor rain these years, except at my word."
² Then the word of the LORD came to him, saying,

To possess the gates of the mountains we will possess first, the dominion mandate to make irreversible decrees like Elijah. Elijah was very confident of being the carrier of the power of GOD that he issued a decree only him alone can reverse.

Job 22:28 (KJV)
²⁸Thou shalt also decree a thing, and it shall be established unto thee: and the light shall shine upon thy ways.

GOD is training those that he will use to make decrees, not as Medo-Persian empire decrees which were many times annulled by divine mandate.

Daniel 4:17 (KJV)
¹⁷This matter is by the decree of the watchers, and the demand

by the word of the holy ones: to the intent that the living may know that the most High ruleth in the kingdom of men, and giveth it to whomsoever he will, and setteth up over it the basest of men. KJV

GOD want the company of watchmen who can stand to shut the heavens, cause famine, make decrees and rule by their words.

Micah 4:1 (KJV)
¹But in the last days it shall come to pass, <u>that the mountain of the house of theLORD shall be established in the top of the muntains, and it shall be exalted above the hills;</u> and people shall flow unto it.

GOD in His infinite mercy has laid for us a sound framework and an everlasting foundation through His words that the realization and emancipation in the mountain of Religion that the church will arise and will gain victories upon the other mountains of influence. The scriptures quoted above was, a repeat of the opening text in Chapter one page one.   It was Prophet Isaiah's prophecy in Isa. 2:2. The contents were the same and even words to words in context. It should be seen as a renewed emphasis that the victory at this mountain of Religion transcends to other mountains.

For another mountain to be established on top of an existing one means-to be superimposed, overwhelmed or dominated by an emerging mountain. It is one thing to be established but another thing to be exalted above the hills. In this period of dispensational grace, we should not only see the LORD's mountain established but see them exalted above the godless and Babylonian systems. This process can be actualized by exercising our dominion mandate over the mountains.

Understanding the mandate and our roles which

these mountains plays in the contest of the destiny of nations, tribes and kingdoms will be a vital means in equipping the church to her apostolic and prophetic position in the present and future dispensation. Unfortunately, this generation has chosen to be more secular, more physical and more factual in principle rather than being more spiritual indeed.

Many treatise in the market or work place ministries are written or being written on transformation on the 7 mountains of influence, this, I believe is a practical approach towards possessing the mountains. Of all the mountains that are mentioned, many people tend to focus on the mountain of Media as the executive arm of the kingdom of darkness and as a veritable tool towards influencing the other mountains.

We should not make this mistake in this era to believe that training alone will be enough towards possessing the mountains. Neither should we think that prayers alone will be enough. This mandate over the mountains will be established by combination of many factors. These factors are: **Training and Preparation, Investigation, Contest and Possession and Dominion**.

The truth is that the Mountain of Religion is the most important and decisive of all the mountains. Understanding of the relevance and the role of this mountain will be the pivot in the process of deposing, subduing and dominating the mountains of influence.

We have taught the church that there is a need to raise, and disciple kingdom conscious believers in preparation towards possessing the mountains. We forgot that we are contending with a kingdom which understands the place of spiritual warfare in exercising control and dominion in every facet of endeavor.

Consider the differences between these scriptures:

Genesis 1:28 (KJV)

[28] And God blessed them, and God said unto them, Be fruitful, and multiply, and replenish the earth, and subdue it: and have dominion over the fish of the sea, and over the fowl of the air, and over every living thing that moveth upon the earth.

Verse 28 as stated above confers executive mandate and power to Adam and his wife. There were threefold responsibilities and a double fold mandate. The initial but essential factor was that first of all things, GOD blessed them before the conferment of the powers. The blessing of GOD empowers the recipient above everyone and everything.

Genesis 9:1-2 (NIV)

[1] Then God blessed Noah and his sons, saying to them, "Be fruitful and increase in number and fill the earth. [2] The fear and dread of you will fall upon all the beasts of the earth and all the birds of the air, upon every creature that moves along the ground, and upon all the fish of the sea; they are given into your hands.

What went wrong here? GOD stopped halfway. The original mandate was withdrawn. Man was only given a threefold responsibility without the two fold mandate. He rather replaced them with fear and dread. These are what the Hittites are using on the mountain of Media to intimidate the world and to perpetuate their own advancement.

Prayer Points

• Pray and ask GOD to help you to discover your talents and other hidden talents.

• Pray that GOD will pass you through a special

training process.

- That through this process you will function extraordinarily on your own mountain of influence.

- Ask GOD to draft you into His own team and also help you to raise another team in preparation for a total takeover.

- Pray the LORD to take train you and bring you into Babylonia system by His wisdom.

- Pray earnestly for impartation of the kingdom mandate in order to exercise dominion on the mountains.

- Pray for the kingdom authority in order to depose the enemies on all the seven mountains.

Chapter Eight

TRAINING AND PREPARATION

This emerging army that the LORD will use in this time of divinely orchestrated conflict for a total takeover of the seven Mountains, there will be formal and informal training of the enlisted men. There are different types of enlistment:

Impressment

Impressment was a method of recruiting able-bodied men for military service, particularly in times of war. It is usually carried out by press gangs. Impressment could involve any means necessary, from violent physical kidnapping to offering so many free drinks that the men were too drunk to realize that they had been involuntarily signed. The new "recruits" were usually impressed in towns and villages near the coast and were paid "the king's allowance" for their involuntary service.

Conscription

This is the system of compulsory enrollment of men and women into the armed forces. Conscripts are distinguished from volunteers and professionals, as well as from mercenaries, who offer their service to any government solely for pay. Conscripts may be called to serve in time of peace in order to train for war; they may be called into uniform in time of emergency. In the United States, conscription is popularly called "the draft" and, by legislative enactment, Selective Service.

Volunteers

Non-conscripted army: an army that relies on recruiting people who enlist voluntarily, rather than conscripting recruits by law.

Mercenaries

Mercenaries are soldiers who receive pay for their services, especially as distinguished from soldiers who owe military service to their nation. Historically, mercenaries were often foreigners, rather than citizens or even residents of the nation for which they fought, and the name has now come to mean only foreign auxiliaries. In the American Revolution Great Britain used Hessian mercenaries to fight against the colonists. The use of mercenaries ended in Europe for the most part with the French Revolution, when their place was taken by national standing armies. The Foreign Legion has existed as a mercenary unit in the French army since 1831.

Foreign Legion

A section of army consisting of foreign volunteers: a section of an army consisting of foreign volunteers, especially that of the French army.

Selection is a Compulsory Process

Considering the levels of training most of the above mentioned armed forces undergoes in order to bring victories and trophies to their nations. The LORD will enlist some people in the reminiscent manner as He did with Amos and Elisha.

Amos 7:14-15

[14]Then answered Amos, and said to Amaziah, I was no prophet, neither was I a prophet's son; but I was an herdsman, and a gatherer of sycomore fruit: [15] And the LORD took me as I followed the flock, and the LORD said unto me, Go, prophesy unto my people Israel.

The LORD is a master planner. He abhors vacuum. GOD cannot depose a people to create a vacuum. GOD told Israel that in possessing the (promised) land, it will be little by little.

The Training is a Process
Exodus 23:29-30 (NIV)

[29]But I will not drive them out in a single year, because the land would become desolate and the wild animals too numerous for you. [30]Little by little I will drive them out before you, until you have increased enough to take possession of the land.

GOD's grand design was to drive the Amorites away through His terror, confusion and hornet. He insisted that their eventual overthrow will be gradual. In order to avoid a vacuum that will arise from the victories, the displacements will be gradual. The reasons were that they were very few and that wild beasts will multiply as a result of the vacuum that will be created and turn against them.

God could not send rain after creation simply because there was no man to till the earth. He sent only mist to garnish the face of the earth. It is to be done little by little. GOD cannot give us the mountains of the Amorites if there are not enough people to take over.

Genesis 2:5-6 (NASU)

[5]For the Lord God had not sent rain upon the earth, and there was no man to cultivate the ground. [6]But a mist used to rise from the earth and water the whole surface of the ground.

The Need for Dedicated Trained Team

Abraham had 318 fighting men. Moses had 72 elders. We need a great team in this coming dispensation. Every great man and woman of substance has their own trained team. Organizations and church groups have theirs. GOD is indeed recruiting his people.

David had a four hundred man fighting force. Besides, there were David's thirty mighty men. These men who became exceptionally excellent in their training as a team.

Genesis 14:14-15 (NIV)

14 When Abram heard that his relative had been taken captive, he called out the 318 trained men born in his household and went in pursuit as far as Dan. 15 During the night Abram divided his men to attack them and he routed them, pursuing them as far as Hobah, north of Damascus.

Even at such medieval period, GOD led Abraham to train men who were born in his own household. He taught them combatant warfare. It would have been a preposterous doom if Abraham had raised nobody. The team was kept together in his house. A winning team is a united team who are kept together. They live together, work together, reason together, war together and excise together.

Gideon had a workforce of 300 men. He did great exploits with them, when he was old the Bible did not informed us why his men did not outlive him. We saw that when Samson manifested, he could neither inherit any remnant of the three hundred men. He neither trained his own army nor worked with any. He rather raised 300 foxes and used them against the Philistines. The resultant effect was inferno in the philistine's farmland with the foxes. Great men who fail to train willing vessels will eventually find willing foxes.

Dangers of Not Having a Trained Team
Judges 15:4-5(NIV)

⁴So he went out and caught three hundred foxes and tied them tail to tail in pairs. He then fastened a torch to every pair of tails, ⁵lit the torches and let the foxes loose in the standing grain of the Philistines. He burned up the shocks and standing grain, together with the vineyards and olive groves.

Hardship in the Training Process

The training will be embodied with hardship which, will be orchestrated by GOD Himself. The terrorists are subjected willingly on their volition; to pass through the excruciating pain and hardship in order to be trained for their masters.

A few of them do die in the hardship and horrendous pains that are associated with the trainings. Thus they die for their master and perish eternally. Our LORD made it known that he who tends to preserve his life will lose it but he who offers his as a sacrifice will be saved.

John 12:25 (NIV)

²⁵The man who loves his life will lose it, while the man who hates his life in this world will keep it for eternal life.

The level of their obedience to the course, their dedication and patriotism are unconditionally unquestionable. Apostle Paul adjured his son in the LORD Timothy to endure hardship as a good soldier.

2 Timothy 2:3 (KJV)

³Thou therefore endure hardness, as a good soldier of Jesus Christ.

The world of today is repulsive to hardship which is called chastisement. It is an essential ingredient in a person of destiny. Many years of training in the wilderness was what made Moses, Isaiah, John de Baptist, David, and many others.

Understanding and Dealing with Babylon

There are many mountains that are inhabited by the Babylonians of our time. Babylon as a system is heavily fortified with what we call Babylonian structures which carries their tested and proven infrastructures. There is economic and political Babylon. The concept of Babylon is the same concept of the seven mountains. Their systems are heavily impermeable, impenetrable and impregnable to strangers. They are usually resistant to change and can never be open to non-adherents of the system. No one can gate-crash easily. How can we enter into Babylon? The LORD commanded.

Micah 4:10 (KJV)

10 Be in pain, and labour to bring forth, O daughter of Zion, like a woman in travail: for now shalt thou go forth out of the city, and thou shalt dwell in the field, and thou shalt go even to Babylon; there shalt thou be delivered; there the Lord shall redeem thee from the hand of thine enemies.

Kingdom Seed are Needed in the Babylonian System

The command is a strategic counsel. We need to train men who will be heavily burdened as David, men who will migrate from the comfort zones of their cities and dwell in discomfort in the fields. Men who will enter Babylon are those who are determined to join the system and learn all the intricacies and rudiments of Babylon.

The LORD promised that whosesoever that enters Babylon will be deliverance inside the system.

The Training is For Total for Transformation.

The training that Moses got in the house of Jethro was enough to purge him of the destructive zeal in Egypt. It is not only the zeal but the Tradition, Culture and the religion of Metaphysics. Moses was a first class graduate of Memphis University in Egypt. He learnt all the magic of the

Egyptians. We need men who had been in those acts. We have got many of them. We need to learn these from them:

- What they use to do to hijack the destinies other business men?

- What kind of sacrifice that gave them such undue advantage?

- What made them to have such dominion in the market places?

Acts 7:22 (NIV)
²²Moses was educated in all the wisdom of the Egyptians and was powerful in speech and action.

He wouldn't have led them beyond the Red sea nor would have done much with murmuring-Israel almost in every situation in the wilderness. The royal training he got was to prepare him for a royal life in the palace. But wilderness experience is to prepare a person of destiny to triumph above the mountains and hills in the wilderness.

Benefits of Hard Trainings

Going through sad experience is actually what makes a person of destiny unshakeable whenever he/she faces great challenges. Those who abhor chastisement would mostly absolve frustration. The essential and additional strength to push forward will be lost when the chips are down. The professional boxers, footballers, wrestlers and great sports men and women are not made in the rings or fields. They are made in the training rooms. Get all the trainings that are required to make you a champion.

The military trainings that soldiers undergo are harder as one specializes in one tactical operation or the other. The Marines of United States is a case study. They are trained to survive in extreme harsh conditions. They could go for days without food or water. These days Christians are no more interested in fasting and prayers. We have declassified fasting as abstaining from one meal in a day.

The standard of GOD in the bible has not changed. The men of signs and wonders yesterday and today are men of prayer, fasting righteousness. If we can come back to that foundation of power, we will begin to manifest the kingdom power. Then, the mountains will begin to shift at our command.

1 Thessalonians 2:9-10 (NIV)
⁹ Surely you remember, brothers, our toil and hardship; we worked night and day in order not to be a burden to anyone while we preached the gospel of God to you. ¹⁵ During the night Abram divided his men to attack them and he routed them, pursuing them as far as Hobah, north of Damascus.

He who must take over the mountains must not wait to be fed by others or be provided for. He must depend on Eternal GOD, work out a means of sustainability while the journey progresses.

To keep one's head going in every situation is a challenge to all of us. We must be determined to keep our heads above the reach of sins, compromises and worldliness. To endure hardship is obligatory even in the course of discharge of our ministerial responsibilities.

Timothy 4:5 (NIV)
⁵But you, keep your head in all situations, endure hardship, do the work of an evangelist, discharge all the duties of your ministry.

The Training is an Act of Love

It is an act of love from GOD that He tries us in His love with hardships. If He passed Abraham, Isaac and Jacob through such excruciating trainings, He will pass every one through a similar process. All finished products are passed through multiple transformational processes.

The emerging kingdom seeds are those that will allow GOD on one hand and avail themselves on the other hand to be trained the hard way.

I came into the church auditorium which one of senior friends presides over as the senior Pastor. I was drawn to a golden nugget on the altar with inscription,

> *'Little prayer little power*
> *More prayer more power*
> *Much prayer much power'*

My spirit was drawn automatically to the wordings and it became a turning point in my prayer life. The ministers, prophets and apostle who moved mountains in the previous and present generations were men of faith who spent much times in the presence of the LORD. Take a decision today and begin to spend much of your time in prayers and see how you would not rule your world through power of GOD.

Consistency is the Watch Word
James 5:17-18 (NIV)

[17]Elijah was a man just like us. He prayed <u>earnestly</u> that it would not rain, and it did not rain on the land for three and a half years. [18]Again he prayed, and the heavens gave rain, and the earth produced its crops.

The underlined word <u>earnestly</u> means fervently and consistently. To understand it better consider the following definitions:

1. **serious and solemn:** intensely or excessively serious and grave in manner or attitude.

    *   an earnest expression.
    *   earnest discussions about privacy and propriety.

2. done in deeply sincere way: undertaken or made in a spirit of deep sincerity and conviction, or with deep feeling. (Source: Microsoft® Encarta® 2009 © 1993-2008).

Prayers Must be Fervent and Effective

Therefore Elijah did not just say a word of prayer once and went home to sleep. He continually was renewing his mandatory decrees. He was insistent in prayers it must not rain. He was reminding GOD to honor the word he spoke in His name. He has never ignored to speak to the heavens to withhold rain. He presented himself as the representative of heaven in that matter. And that only his word can reverse the decree.

Daniel 1:8, 9, 12 (NIV)

8But Daniel resolved not to defile himself with the royal food and wine, and he asked the chief official for permission not to defile himself this way. 9Now God had caused the official to show favor and sympathy to Daniel, 12 "Please test your servants for ten days: Give us nothing but vegetables to eat and water to drink. 13Then compare our appearance with that of the young men who eat the royal food.

We need men with these types of resolve as Daniel and his colleagues did. Esther resolved to perish for the sake of her nation but GOD preserved her. Moses refused to be identified as the son of Pharaoh's daughter. He rather preferred to escape to condition of servitude in order to fulfill his calling as a deliverer.

Hebrews 11:24-25 (NIV)

24By faith Moses, when he had grown up, refused to be known as the son of Pharaoh's daughter. 25He chose to be mistreated along with the people of God rather than to enjoy the pleasures of sin for a short time.

GOD loves us, that is why He needs such attributes of patience to be formed in us. He knows that men are impatient naturally.

Hebrews 12:7-9 (NKJV)
⁷If you endure chastening, God deals with you as with sons; for what son is there whom a father does not chasten? ⁸But if you are without chastening, of which all have become partakers, then you are illegitimate and not sons.

Prayer Points

- Pray GOD to set you apart for special and peculiar assignments.

- Ask GOD to define your role in the kingdom army, and train you to specialize in your own responsibilities.

- Ask GOD to confirm your present calling.

- Pray for the grace to be relevant and fruitful in every season all the days of your life.

- Pray for total obedience and submission throughout any time of hardship through trainings.

Chapter Nine

SURVEY AND INVESTIGATION

Causes of Rise and Fall of Kingdoms

It is very imperative to know that great kingdoms have risen at certain times and seasons. One thing made them great and another brought them down. Some of them were traceable in museums and in history books. Some of them were reduced to a miniature country and state.

We cannot help but be impressed by the great empires of the past. The Babylonian Empire ruled the Middle East, and the armies of Nebuchadnezzar were unstoppable. The mighty Roman Empire lasted for 500 years, before falling to the Vandals and the Heruli. World War II saw the Blitzkrieg expansion of the Third Reich across Europe and North Africa. Hitler's ambitions included conquest of the Soviet Union, but he failed, and Allied armies pummeled mighty Germany into a rubble heap. Can any nation or empire long endure? Can the U.S. last much longer as a superpower? What does the Bible say about the future of kingdoms, empires and nations? Does God have a say in what will happen? What are the lessons of history—and Scripture—and the warnings they portend for Western civilization?

The Union of Soviet Socialist Republics consisted of

15 republics and one-sixth of the world's land surface, or 2.5 times the area of the U.S. This great superpower reveled in its Communist ideology; it fought for the hearts of nations all over the world and lost. On November 9, 1989, the symbol of its subjugation of Eastern Europe, the Berlin wall, came tumbling down.

Now, this once-mighty power has shattered into 15 struggling nation-states, with 12 tied together in the Commonwealth of Independent States. Who could have predicted the fall of this great superpower? A small group of biblically based Christians did understand that Eastern Europe would eventually escape the iron grip of the Soviet Union. How could they have known that? Bible prophecy predicted the rise of another great superpower, called the Beast in the book of Revelation. Nearly 50 years ago, Herbert W. Armstrong wrote that East Germany would be rejoined to West Germany, and that Russia "will be forced to relinquish her control over Hungary, Czechoslovakia and parts of Austria" (**Source: Plain Truth, April 1952, p. 16**).

Daniel was a man of prayer, wisdom, knowledge and understanding. When it was approaching the time of the end of Babylonian captivity, GOD raised multitude of intercessors simultaneously of which Daniel was one of the notable intercessors. These, we can call remnant company. Daniel's burden was unbearably expressed like that of Nehemiah, after he read this account through his research lifestyle.

Understanding the Causes of Fall of Great Nations
Daniel 9:2 (KJV)
2In the first year of his reign I Daniel understood by books the number of the years, whereof the word of the Lord came to Jeremiah the prophet, that he would accomplish seventy years in the desolations of Jerusalem.

Our kingdom needs to train spies. Spies are

usually few in number. When Moses sent twelve, it was a disaster. When Joshua sent two it was a success. Nations and kingdoms invest billions of Dollars in intelligence and counter intelligence espionage network. They believe in strategic information gathering, advanced communication and radar monitoring devices. Through these they can pre-empt or undo the enemy strategies.

GOD will raise Issachar army in this dispensation. Unfortunately, the men on the mountains are never perturbed about what the word of the LORD is saying to them. They are always comfortable like, Nebuchadnezzar. Whenever they look at their business empires, they are highly satisfied to attest that their hands have achieved those things. Their hearts are highly and haughtily exalted. They have never read nor understood what Nebuchadnezzar said after his humiliation and restoration.

Daniel 4:17 (KJV)
17This matter is (settled) by the decree of the watchers, and the demand by the word of the holy ones: to the intent that the living may know that the most High ruleth in the kingdom of men, and giveth it to whomsoever he will, and setteth up over it the basest of men.

The Person and Gifts of the Holy Spirit
We have superior advantages in the person and the ministry of the Holy Spirit. Even in the time of Old Testament the superior gifts of revelations has been in operation. Elisha, Moses and many others were proven men of such rare gifts. One perfect example was when the King of Syria was at war with Israel in 2 Kings 6.

Elisha was guiding the Israeli soldiers through his superior revelational knowledge. He actually made void all the military tactical initiatives of Syrians. In effect, the king was sore afraid and thought that there was an informant

within his inner caucus. He queried thus, (**2 Kings 6:11 –
NIV**) *"Will you not tell me which of us is on the side of the
king of Israel?"* He was stunned with the reply he got.

2 Kings 6:12-13 (NIV)
*"None of us, my lord the king," said one of his officers, "but
Elisha, the prophet who is in Israel, tells the king of Israel the
very words you speak in your bedroom."*

My prayer is that the LORD will raise in us and for
us many prophets like Elisha. There are many gifted men in
the reminiscent manner, we need to ask GOD, discover and
harness them for the requisite trainings.

In possessing the mountains, we need Daniels and
Josephs and many more who will have understanding of
the books, the times and the seasons. When Daniel learnt
that he and his three friends were among those that will be
executed by the harsh decree of King Nebuchadnezzar. He
requested a time to enquire of the LORD.

Solutions Must Come from Deeper Revelations
Daniel 2:16-20 (NIV)
*[16]At this, Daniel went in to the king and asked for time, so that
he might interpret the dream for him. [17]Then Daniel returned
to his house and explained the matter to his friends Hananiah,
Mishael and Azariah. [18]He urged them to plead for mercy
from the God of heaven concerning this mystery, so that he and
his friends might not be executed with the rest of the wise men
of Babylon. [19]During the night the mystery was revealed to
Daniel in a vision. Then Daniel praised the God of heaven.*

Spiritual Mapping of the Mountains
We need spiritual and physical survey of the
mountains. Joshua surveyed the land of promise. He wrote
a concise cartographic description of the land. We must
train spiritual cartographers or 'spiritual mapping' experts

according to C. Peter Wagner. Their job description will be to furnish us with spiritual topography of the mountains. In every city we need men that are like the elders at the gate of Jericho. Apostle Paul recognized that the eldership in every city will re order things that are lacking there.

Titus 1:5 (NIV)
⁵The reason I left you in Crete was that you might straighten out what was left unfinished and appoint a elders in every town, as I directed you.

The Need for Proper Eldership

We need to set elders at the gate of every one of our cities and mountains. Thus, the men of the city of Jericho were actually the watchmen at the city gate.

2 Kings 2:19 (NIV)
¹⁹The men of the city said to Elisha, "Look, our lord, this town is well situated, as you can see, but the water is bad and the land is unproductive."

There must be elders at the gate of every city who will watch and pray like the men of Jericho. The sons of the prophets are the watchmen at the gate of the city. This band of seminarians was very knowledgeably sensitive to their environment. They understood from the books as Daniel did. They understood the genesis of the problems in Jericho. They knew that foundation of the multifaceted problems in the land. Joshua cursed the land of Jericho.

The Rebuilders Must Know the Depth of the Foundation
Josh 6:26 (KJV) - *²⁶Cursed be the man before the Lord, that riseth up and buildeth this city Jericho: he shall lay the foundation thereof in his firstborn, and in his youngest son shall he set up the gates of it.*
1 Kings 16:34 (KJV) - *³⁴In his days did Hiel the Bethelite build Jericho: he laid the foundation thereof in Abiram his firstborn, and set up the gates thereof in his youngest son Segub,*

according to the word of the Lord, which he spake by Joshua the son of Nun.

Discerning and Surveying the Topography

These sons of the prophet have understanding of the past and the present. They sought for solution that will endure for many generations.

Joshua sent men to go and survey their inheritances and write it down. We must carry out constant surveys.

Joshua 18:3-4 (NIV)

³So Joshua said to the Israelites: "How long will you wait before you begin to take possession of the land that the Lord, the God of your fathers, has given you? ⁴Appoint three men from each tribe. I will send them out to make a survey of the land and to write a description of it, according to the inheritance of each. Then they will return to me.

Nehemiah the rebuilder is a role model in this understanding. The following scriptures stated emphatically, the ebullient manner by which he conducted his mission discreetly. He went out at night, viewed the walls, took note and understood the level of the damages and desolations.

Nehemiah Views the Wall of Jerusalem
Nehemiah 2:11-16 (NKJV)

¹¹ So I came to Jerusalem and was there three days. ¹²Then I arose in the night, I and a few men with me; I told no one what my God had put in my heart to do at Jerusalem; nor was there any animal with me, except the one on which I rode. ¹³And I went out by night through the Valley Gate to the Serpent Well and the Refuse Gate, and viewed the walls of Jerusalem which were broken down and its gates which were burned with fire. ¹⁴Then I went on to the Fountain Gate and to the King's Pool, but there was no room for the animal under me to pass. ¹⁵So I went up in the night by the valley, and viewed the wall; then I

turned back and entered by the Valley Gate, and so returned.
[16]And the officials did not know where I had gone or what I had
done; I had not yet told the Jews, the priests, the nobles, the
officials, or the others who did the work.

He was a typical example of one who has a combination of both: discernment, surveying, building, networking and espionage experience.

I have never ceased to admire Eli Cohen of the blessed memories. His espionage and intelligence lifestyle is worthy of emulation in these seasons and times.

Cohen was born in Alexandria to a devout Jewish and Zionist family in 1924. His father had moved there from Aleppo in 1914. In January 1947, he chose to enlist in the Egyptian Army as an alternative to paying the prescribed sum all young Jews were supposed to pay, but was declared ineligible on grounds of questionable loyalty. Later that year, he left university and began studying at home after facing harassment by the Muslim Brotherhood. In the years following the creation of Israel, many Jewish families left Egypt. Though his parents and three brothers left for Israel in 1949, Cohen remained to finish a degree in electronics and to coordinate Jewish and Zionist activities. In 1951, following a military coup, an anti-Zionist campaign was initiated, and Cohen was arrested and interrogated over his Zionist activities Cohen took part in various Israeli covert operations in the country during the 1950s, though the Egyptian government could never verify and provide proof of his involvement in Operation Goshen, an Israeli operation to smuggle Egyptian Jews out of the country and resettle them in Israel due to increasing hostility there.

The Mossad recruited Cohen after Director-General Meir Amit, looking for a special agent to infiltrate the Syrian government, came across his name while looking through the agency's files of rejected candidates, after none of the current candidates seemed suitable for the job. For two weeks he was put under surveillance, and was judged suitable for recruitment and training. Cohen was then informed that the Mossad had decided to recruit him, and underwent an intensive, six-month course at the Mossad training school, and his graduate report stated that he had all the qualities needed to become a katsa, or field agent.[4][6]

He was then given a false identity as a Syrian businessman who was returning to the country after living in Argentina. To establish his cover, Cohen moved to Argentina in 1961.

The tactics of Cohen to build relations with Syrian high-ranked politicians, military officials, influential public figures and local foreign diplomacy community, have been carefully masterminded by Mossad. Details of his espionage tactics are classified and most probably would never be revealed to public. Cohen was a genius spy actor and exceeded all expectations of Mossad. He continued his social life as in Argentina, spending a lot of time in cafes listening to political gossip. He also held parties at his home, which turned into orgies for high-placed Syrian ministers, businessmen, and others, who used Eli's apartment "for assignations with various women, including Defense Ministry secretaries, airline hostesses, and Syrian singing stars." At these parties such highly-placed officials would "talk freely of their work and army plans. Eli, who would feign intoxication, remained sober and listened carefully." In addition to providing loans to government officials and acting as an avid host, he was asked for advice by government officials, who were often intoxicated by the alcohol he freely provided. Eli himself was not above the spicier part of a spy's life either. He had seventeen lovers in Syria, all dazzling beauties with a fair degree of family power." Cohen provided an incredible amount of intelligence data to the Israeli Army over a period of four years (1961-1965). Cohen sent intelligence to Israel by radio, secret letters, and occasionally in person, he secretly traveled

*to Israel three times. His most famous achievement was
when he toured the Golan Heights, and collected intelligence
on the Syrian fortifications there. Feigning sympathy for
the soldiers exposed to the sun, Cohen had trees planted at
every position. The trees were used as targeting markers by
the Israeli military during the Six-Day War and enabled
Israel to easily capture the Golan Heights in two days. Cohen
made repeated visits to the southern frontier zone, providing
photographs and sketches of Syrian positions. Cohen learned
of an important secret plan by Syria to create three successive
lines of bunkers and mortars; the Israel Defense Forceswould
otherwise have expected to encounter only a single line.*

*In January 1965, Syrian efforts to find a high-level
mole were stepped up. Using Soviet-made tracking equipment
and assisted by hired Soviet experts, a period of radio silence
was observed, and it was hoped that any illegal transmissions
could be identified. After large amounts of radio interference
were detected and traced to their source, on the 24th of
January, Syrian security officers broke into Cohen's apartment
where he was caught in the middle of transmission to Israel.
The leading figure in the break-in was the head of Syrian
Intelligence, Colonel Ahmed Su'edani - Eli's nemesis.* **(Source:
Wikipedia)**

To do more in this context is to know how, when,
where and what went wrong. Our spiritual warfare in
many nations has been made possible and easier whenever
GOD gives us understanding of the terrain. Whenever am
travelling to any country or city, I do usually spend some
days to Google all the information that could be helpful in
my missions. Above all my dreams and revelations have
always been a great advantage. We need to spend time to
listen to the Holy Spirit.

Besides that, we need to properly access an informed
elder or a gifted remnant who will furnish us with the

dossier of an enclave or institution for proper preparation to takeover.

Job 8:8-11 (NIV)
[8]"Ask the former generations
and find out what their fathers learned,
[9]for we were born only yesterday and know nothing,
and our days on earth are but a shadow.
[10]Will they not instruct you and tell you?
Will they not bring forth words from their understanding?
[11] Can papyrus grow tall where there is no marsh?
Can reeds thrive without water?

Prayer Points

• GOD still speaks in dreams, vision and revelations, ask GOD to speak to you in diverse ways

• Pray that through the access to revelations, that you will have superior advantage over the heathens in every mountain

• Pray that the Holy Spirit will; reveal to you the foundations of all the mountains

• Ask GOD to show you the nature of the controlling powers on all the mountains

• Let us pray that GOD will give us revelation and strategies to overcome the delays on the mountains

Chapter Ten

CONTEST ON THE MOUNTAINS

The Mandate Will Preserve the Burden Bearer

I have lived a life of and taught spiritual warfare as a mainstay in my ministry across the nations of the world. In Africa, we understand the realities of spiritual warfare than our Western counterparts in the ministries. We have been in a continent where life means nothing to many people. Anyone can be killed at any moment. But one thing is certain; a man of divine destiny with GOD cannot die until the purpose of GOD in his is actualized.

David had everything that could lead to his death. Moses was born in a time of unparalleled upheavals, a time of Egyptian male infanticide movement against the Jewry. Yet, he could not be killed. Mordecai and Esther were made manifest to save the Jewry. They could not be killed because of the divine purposes in their lives. I declare to you, *'you cannot die before your time. You will fulfill all the divine purposes in your life in JESUS name'.*

In almost every part of Africa, to decide to live a life of righteousness is like an offense before the eyes of everybody. Patriotism and nationalism has gradually eroded.

Yeast Strategy

In spiritual combat, our prayers are to be seen and

known as yeast in dough of cake or bread. A little leaven which can leaven the whole lump. We need to develop a mountain moving faith. Our prayers towards possessing the mountains should be considered a project. A project is never delivered until it is finished. We need to kick start prayer projects towards the mountains. The following points are the prayer strategies that will help us to initiate prayer strategies over the mountains.

Yeast is a small single-celled fungus that ferments sugars and other carbohydrates and reproduces by budding. These catalysts are the depiction of what our spiritual life should be. It is known in the bible as the little leaven that leavens the whole lump. We should have a contagious prayer life that will influence others and revolutionize a whole system.

Spiritual warfare is a contest between the kingdom of GOD and the kingdom of darkness. We fight for the control of souls of men, resources, and kingship and ruler ship. Also, to wrestle power and the glory of the kingdoms of this world unto the glorious liberty of the sons of GOD.

Mandate Without Authority

GOD forbid that we should be like Samson who rule Israel in his time but was not a ruler.

Judges 15:20 (NLT)
Samson judged Israel for twenty years during the period when the Philistines dominated the land.

GOD allowed and will always allow His people to be trained through certain afflictions and the wars of the inhabitants of the unconquered enemies.

The Trials and Wars are the Training
Judges 3:1-2 (KJV)
¹Now these are the nations which the Lord left, to prove Israel by them, even as many of Israel as had not known all the wars

of Canaan; ²Only that the generations of the children of Israel might know, to teach them war, at the least such as before knew nothing thereof;

Not only that we should learn spiritual warfare but the generations after us will learn the art of war. Our sons and daughters in the LORD including our biological offspring must learn how to wage spiritual wars.

Taking Territories or the Mountains is Biblical
Deuteronomy 3:4-7 (KJV)

⁴And we took all his cities at that time, there was not a city which we took not from them, threescore cities, all the region of Argob, the kingdom of Og in Bashan. ⁵All these cities were fenced with high walls, gates, and bars; beside unwalled towns a great many. ⁶And we utterly destroyed them, as we did unto Sihon king of Heshbon, utterly destroying the men, women, and children, of every city. ⁷But all the cattle, and the spoil of the cities, we took for a prey to ourselves.

We must take over the mountains. We will display the awesome power of GOD through prayers. We must subdue nations and kingdoms through faith. We must fight the good fight of faith. Every believer should see the war as a war against the kingdom of our GOD. We must see the affliction of every believer as the affliction on the Church. We cannot tarry on one mountain for so long. There remain many more mountains to conquer. We must help our brothers on the other mountains to take over. We shall not have rest until the mountains are possessed.

There Will be Speed in Taking Over
Deuteronomy 1:6 (NIV)

⁶The Lord our God said to us in Horeb, "You have stayed long enough at this mountain.

GOD is giving us a charge that the mountains are set before us. What shall we do? The LORD commanded that we should contend with them in the battle. To defend the vows he swore to our father Abraham and his descendants. The command is that we must arise and fight to recover the lost territories. And annex the unconquered ones.

Deuteronomy 1:8 (KJV)
8Behold, I have set the land before you: go in and possess the land which the Lord sware unto your fathers, Abraham, Isaac, and Jacob, to give unto them and to their seed after them.

There are certain kings on our mountains known as Sihon the strong man of Amorites and Heshbon her king. We need to get them overthrown from our mountains. The LORD has already put our dread into their heart, they are already afraid.

Deuteronomy 2:24-25 (KJV)
24Rise ye up, take your journey, and pass over the river Arnon: behold, I have given into thine hand Sihon the Amorite, king of Heshbon, and his land: begin to possess it, and contend with him in battle. 25This day will I begin to put the dread of thee and the fear of thee upon the nations that are under the whole heaven, who shall hear report of thee, and shall tremble, and be in anguish because of thee.

A Great Effort in Futility
The religious mountain is the most potent of the mountains, we must not liken the church as part of the mountain of religion but to see it having been established and exalted above the mountains. There was a November 29, 1979 Islamic conference in Abuja, Nigeria. It was decided that Nigeria will be Islamized and that governance must never be compromised to the Christians. It is their right to rule.

To capture and Islamize Nigeria is victory for Islam in the continent. Islam must not be seen as a religious organization alone. It is one of the executive arms of Lucifer. It employs all the overt and covert strategies to be feared. In addition, it employs clandestine and terrorist hard lines to execute its mandate.

The Need for Priests and Counselors

Companies and Parastatals owned by Indians, Lebanese, Muslims and occult men understand the mysteries in strategic praying and prophetic actions. All their companies have their own priests, apostles and prophets. They hire their services always and depend on their counsels and predictions. Oftentimes, they are given shares in their companies or paid salaries and tithes. All is to secure their blessings in their so called prayers/ sacrifices.

Government. politics and politicking have become one of the strongest mountains to ascend. In Africa, the issue of governance has caused about 99% of all the wars than any other event.

Prayer Points

- Command that you will be transform into kingdom yeasts, salt and light of the world.

- Declare and say, 'Oh LORD you who led Israel to conquer the Seven mountains of the Amorites and the Canaanites, help me to conquer my mountains.

- Perhaps, we are dwelling (working) on a mountain that is rotten. You need to understand the gravity of the rottenness and start a process of identification and repentance of all the sins in the system.

- Identify various negative covenants and destroy them through your priestly authority.

95

- Take up your bible and start making prophetic declarations on the mountains.

- Attack through the judgment of the word of GOD, the negative structures that have resisted godliness in our educational system.

- Depose the agent of darkness and call for the emergence of kingdom leaders in the educational who will rewrite the school curriculum.

- Pray for credible election, electoral process and election of godly candidates in position of authority.

Chapter Eleven

POSSESSION AND DOMINION

The Five-fold Mandates

Possession and dominion is wholly scriptural. The five-fold of GOD's given mandate to man were very specific. **Genesis 1:28-29 (KJV)**

And God blessed them, and God said unto them, Be fruitful, and multiply, and replenish the earth, and subdue it: and have dominion over the fish of the sea, and over the fowl of the air, and over every living thing that moveth upon the earth. 29And God said, Behold, I have given you every herb bearing seed, which is upon the face of all the earth, and every tree, in the which is the fruit of a tree yielding seed; to you it shall be for meat.

That means that a proper understanding of the above mentioned mandates are our essential heritage from GOD. The last two mandates are where the Church has got it wrong. We can be fruitful, multiply and replenish. The issue of subduing and establishing dominion is the end point.

A Three-fold Mandate
Genesis 8:17 (KJV)
[17]..Breed abundantly in the earth, and be fruitful, and multiply upon the earth.

After the fall of man, those two most essential

mandates were withdrawn. There were only recovered totally through our LORD's victory on the cross. It is written in the following scriptures:

The Essential Way to Power and Authority
Philippians 2:8-10 (NIV)
⁸And being found in appearance as a man,
he humbled himself
and became obedient to death —
even death on a cross!
⁹Therefore God exalted him to the highest place
and gave him the name that is above every name,
¹⁰ that at the name of Jesus every knee should bow,
in heaven and on earth and under the earth,

And in the book of Mathew it is stated after the resurrection of our LORD JESUS. The authority was not given until he had earned it on the cross.
Matthew 28:18-19 (NIV)
¹⁸Then Jesus came to them and said, "All authority in heaven and on earth has been given to me. ¹⁹Therefore go and make disciples of all nations,

In many parts of other scripture they are written *'behold I give power and authority'*. This dominion mandate is a vital aspect of our kingdom wherewith we must showcase the manifold wisdom of GOD. Unfortunately, we have ignorantly allowed the heathen to take advantage of us and have been manifesting false dominion. I declare e to whomever that is reading this piece 'receive a dominion mandate in JESUS name.

Mountain of Family

A strong family unit is an antidote against all the ungodliness of the world. GOD gave a report card of Abraham's family life. Can GOD testify of us?

Abraham's family
Gen 18:19 (NKJV)
[19]For I have known him (Abraham), in order that he may command his children and his household after him, that they keep the way of the Lord, to do righteousness and justice,

I and my wife regulate the television program that our children will watch. This is peculiar at certain stages of their growth and development. We determine which party they will attend. We teach them basic dress codes. Studying their scriptures are basic statute and precepts. We made sure that we are available to them as their best friends. I made sure that prayers are made daily unto them from conception (while they are in the womb). I and my wife do lay our hands on her womb daily.

Whenever I am away I will instruct her to lay her hands on her womb while I speak into their lives through the telephones. Later, we adopted (as taught by one of my mentors) to select a day respectively in a week to pray for our children. The prayers includes: their education, ministry, marriage, friends and everything related to their prophetic upbringing.

In our daily family altar of prayers, all the children are brought out to join the prayers. Even when they are asleep we lay them in their colts and couches. The new born babies are laid on their beds in the middle of the sitting room while the prayers go on. If we do these and many more positively we will no doubt conquer the mountain of family. I and my wife are very close, we share everything together. We make out time for leisure trips and outings periodically.

Mountain of Education

In many African nations, the standard of education has gradually eroded to the level that our university degree certificates have become mere papers. Yet, we have among them many lectures, professors and seasoned administrators that profess CHRIST as born again kingdom citizens. While the others are taking bribe, sleeping with our sons and daughters to 'sort' them out, my question is where are the influences of the kingdom citizens?

Christian Universities beyond the Christians

Many Christian universities have been floated since the last two decades but, none of them without exception, are within the reach of an average Christian family. It is founded for the bourgeois class. My question is, "If the brilliant Christian scholars are denied admission into the universities owned sometimes by the church which they and their parents have been members from birth and have contributed both financially and otherwise; what is the hope of their salvation in the same church?"

Notwithstanding, the impact of the Christian schools in the present dispensation cannot be overemphasized. One could recall how the defunct government of late general Murtala Mohamed (the military head of state in Nigeria took the whole Christian schools and converted all to government schools, that was how the foundation of moral decadence was laid to eclipse the nation.

Education Without GOD

For many years now, the Supreme Court in United States ruled against the use of Bibles and prayers in public schools. Thus, ever since the ruling, the rate of crime in public schools has increased in geometric proportion.

The foundation of education we inherited in Africa is supposed to be great. All the schools were established by foreign Christian missionary organizations. But, when we took over from the missionaries when we got independence, we eroded the very essence of the founding organizations. In some nations, the government acquired all the schools. The bible has counseled thus,

Getting it Right From the Cradle
Proverbs 22:6 (NIV)
⁶Train a child in the way he should go,
and when he is old he will not turn from it.

We need to float educational institutions that will mold our children to into a formidable force with Christian values and virtues. Not just children with negative upbringings. Our children are to be brought forth with travailing sacrifices until Christ is fully formed in them. We need to broker several covenants between our children and GOD.

Galatians 4:19-20 (NIV)
¹⁹My dear children, for whom I am again in the pains of childbirth until Christ is formed in you, ²⁰how I wish I could be with you now and change my tone, because I am perplexed about you!

Our children need our presence. We must work harder to see that the teachings of Christ are fully formed in them. There is a great exploit that has been demonstrated on this mountain by someone I know of. He is a Nigerian who got a miraculous teaching job in London. This lady will always come early, pray for a few minutes before the arrival of other workers. She will read her bible and pray over both seats and for the children. She will equally pray with the children together before the teachings of the day.

During the examination, her class performed beyond many expectations. Within one academic session her students have been known as, the best behaved class. Gossips began to grow that she has turned her class to church. One thing was certain her class which was most undesirable has become envy. Her fame rose tremendously in the school. She became a heroin overnight.

At the inception of another academic year, some Muslims parents came with their wards to be admitted into her class. They were informed that the teacher use to teach her class bible and how to pray. Their replies were whatever you did to the children of my neighbors please do that to my kids. Afterwards, other schools began to scramble to hire her. Why? She has subdued the mountain of education.

Mountain of Politics:
The Rot and Satanism in Politics

Politics in Africa is a different ball game as regards their Western counterparts. Electioneering campaigns are more spiritually done than physical. To understand this in detail, one should be prepared to make a book of many volumes. I have been involved in mobilizing the church in different nations of Africa for prayers during their years of election. I have come to the realities that to win any election in the third world especially in Africa is beyond the physical campaign.

Diabolism in Election

During the election year in African countries, the cases of human sacrifice are more salient than ever. Mysterious disappearances of people are usually on the increase. Special types of human beings are in high demand for sacrifices during the period. Albinos, hunch-backs, virgins and newborn babies are highly sought after. Many Witch Doctors are flown into the countries from other witchcraft stronghold nations for such purposes.

These diabolical candidates understand that to win the election is **do or die affairs**. They can't afford to pay such prizes and lose the election. They do go into marriage covenants with different spirits for the same purposes. They understand that the world and the marketplace go to the highest bidder. Therefore, election seats goes to the highest bidders. These sacrifices are carried out at strategic times and seasons. Their names and influences are programmed in the atmosphere, moon, sun and stars. They deploy all the forces of creation to campaign for them.

Some hitherto, unpopular candidates will unexpectedly appear from behind the scene. Suddenly, the godly and the popular ones will begin to wane down. When these start to happen it's possible that much sacrifices have been done.

The Effect of Witchcraft in Politics

Whenever there is undue frenzy at the mention of their names let it be known that much sorceries may have been done. People are bewitched to follow and flow to them in an unexplainable circumstance. Most times they are taken to ancient shrines (altars) to be ministered unto. It could be at some of the so-called UNESCO adopted sites mostly in Africa or elsewhere. These sites are demonic shrines/altars. United Nations, which is a godless body that has been hijacked by the New Age Movement, has it as satanically designed strategies to preserve such demonic places for their nefarious activities.

In many occasions, several Islamic Marabous are employed to entrench the much needed enchantments and incantations to bewitch a nation or territories for their principal. In many third- world nations, most of the wickedness that are being perpetrated on the economy through the governance came as a result of the demonic spirits that were imported by the politicians and rulers mostly during the election campaigns. Others were imported at the times of unpopular governments in order to use such powers to suppress the nation to their will.

Various Negative Government Foundations

During the military regime in Nigeria, so much of those transactions were done by one of the ubiquitous dictators. In order to remain in power for 2 decades, he imported some Islamic Marabous from Saudi Arabia. Firstly, they brought 1000 mice, used tiny pins to pierce their eyes and bind their mouth. They dug the earth and buried them in the presidential palace. With much sacrifices and rituals they proclaimed that 'whenever these mice open their eyes; so shall the peoples' eyes be open', in order words, it means that the eyes of the nation will never be open to challenge the government schemes to elongate her tenure.

Secondly, hyenas were imported, bound with chains and buried in the presidential palace in a bid to bind the strength and the power of the nation from protesting against the government. One particular episode that happened during the first term of political independence was that the British colonial lords insisted that the premiership must be ceded to the northern people who were mostly Muslims and were much educationally backward. The Prime Minister was selected from that region.   As he tasted the power, he invited the same class of Marabous who did the following satanic prophetic action. They brought bean seedlings of the planting season of the year. The seeds were buried in the old presidential palace with a declaration that *'whenever these seeds germinate, then shall the Christian in Nigeria produce the Head of State'.*

In almost all the developing countries, human sacrifices are still being done in all the presidential palaces. To ascend to certain political office, one must be forced to enter into one cult of fraternity or the order in order to acquire political power. Most of the times, they were forced to swear to an oaths of allegiance to certain deities and

104

individuals.

The Strong Gates of Politics

Some new political entrants are being frustrated from winning any election in certain countries on the grounds that they don't have the so-called godfathers or that they refused to swear an oath to some strange gods or to be initiated into one of the grand fraternities. Even when it's obvious that they will or had won the election they will be denied the mandate.

In some cases in Nigeria, in addition to the oath of allegiance, a candidate will write a signed advance resignation letter without a date on it. This letter will be given to the so called sponsors or godfathers. This will empower them to publish the resignation letter and chase the person(s) out of office. These are done with the help of the police.

A major horrible factor is the advent of the Illuminati and Freemason cults. All the wars in ever fought and are being fought in Africa, have always been the handiwork of these groups. The only reason is that GOD made Africa the richest continent in terms of natural resources. To control the resource is the reason for all the wars.

In Democratic Republic of Congo, for example, over 8.5 million lives have been wasted, since 1999 till date by the Western Nations through these cultic organizations. The figure is far beyond what the Jewry lost during the world war era. No news media has carried it. Western Nations are silent on the issue. Our major sin, according to them, is that GOD made a mistake to endow the nations with such great wealth.

The mountain of politics is greatly strategic and as such it cannot exist without the help of Religious Mountain. The above mentioned transactions were done in a country.

It took concerted efforts of seasoned and informed Intercessors to revoke and reverse those covenants before the first Christian was elected president of this great nation.

In the Mountain of Politics especially in Africa and third world countries; it goes beyond what we know in capacity building and establishment of structures of administration. The reasons why we are difficult is that the spiritual atmosphere is so fortified; that even if an angel of GOD is made to sit on the throne of government, the spiritual structures will contend earnestly to frustrate him.

The insight into the politicking and politics in Africa is beyond normal comprehension. The reasons for these explanations are: to equip the Church to be battle-ready to contend, overthrow and overcome the powers that be in the mountain of politics. Without the prosecution of spiritual warfare on this mountain, the preparations to take over the mountains will be a mere figment of imagination. Apostle Paul told his son Timothy:

1 Timothy 1:18-19 (NKJV)
[18]This charge I commit to you, son Timothy, according to the prophecies previously made concerning you, that by them you may wage the good warfare, [19] having faith and a good conscience, which some having rejected, concerning the faith have suffered shipwreck,

Surely, many prophecies are gone forth concerning the takeover of the mountains. But, we must contend with the occupants by waging a good warfare. Timothy was not asked to go and sleep and wait for the fulfillment of the prophecies, he was asked to wage a good warfare.

Prayer Points

- In this dispensation, we need kingdom mandate to overcome the lesser negative kingdom. mandates, pray for the deposit of the dominion mandate.

- Repent of the way we may have aided and abated the rot on the family mountain.

- Command the power of witchcraft to collapse from all the mountains.

- Ask GOD to show us the way to acquire the dominion mandate.

- Let us begin to proclaim the word of the LORD over the mountains saying **'let there be light on the seven mountains'** name the mountains one by one.

Chapter Twelve

POSSESSION AND DOMINION 2

Mountain of Business

It is the responsibilities of the Church to prayerfully disciple the emerging mega kingdom businessmen and women that will establish dominion in the market place. The major bane militating against many potential businesses in Africa is lack of human capital. The Church is yet to grasp the need to float training institutes for business people. Our generation can't depend on Harvard Business School. We can float a better one through the Church. However, we need to encourage business men and women to avail themselves the opportunities and multiple professional business trainings. We cannot make much difference until we understand the rudiments and modus operandi of world businesses and their systems.

The Rot in Professional Businesses

A proper look at professional businesses will marvel a right thinking kingdom citizen of the great rots in some sectors. The mountain of business as regards medical practices, pharmacy and nutrition is jeopardy. A critical look at the Hippocratic vow will convince you that the origin of medical science was meant to be discharged with in-depth understanding of nutrition. Dr. Hippocrates of

Greece who founded modern medicine tied the profession negatively with idolatry and positively with nutrition. One positive insight was that healthcare deliveries will be discharged with proper knowledge of nutrition (www. hippocraticvow.com).

Today, it appears that the aspect of nutrition is an offence to medical profession. Mafias have hijacked the food industries. The entire society is encouraged to eat or drink to die. Food processing is not being monitored, while fast food has become the mainstay of our menu. Life expectancy will hit ground zero if the kingdom professionals fail to manifest to take over the mountain of healthcare deliveries. I have seen and heard many sicknesses reversed with balanced nutrition adherence. Why should the medical sciences be bound to orthodox, artificial and synthetic drugs? Should we not refer back to all the biblical injunctions about the benefits of fruit and vegetable?

I am always bewildered whenever I watch the advert jingles of our beverages and the so called fruit juices. We are always boldly told that it contains no sugar and no artificial supplements. The health authorities know these lies but will ignore all. This generation and the subsequent ones are doomed unless; something new happens, we need a national and global nutrition policy.

We need nutritionists with sound biblical authority. GOD established an order for a balanced heath care delivery with fruits, vegetable and natural herbs. Daniel was a man of deep understanding. He implored the king's personal assistant to allow him and his friends a ten day period to eat only vegetables. At the end of the ten days, it was stated:
Daniel 1:12, 15 (NIV)
[12]*"Please test your servants for ten days: Give us nothing but vegetables to eat and water to drink. [15]At the end of the ten days they looked healthier and better nourished than any of*

the young men who ate the royal food.

I counsel anyone that is hooked to just fast food to start a process of withdrawal. It's neither good for the children or to adults. Fast foods lead to fast deaths. I challenge the nutritionists, medical doctors and health professional to return back to the very foundations of longevity. Our ancestors lived longer than us. Of all the social and scientific amenities, how come that we are having shorter live span?

Muslims and Business

In my country, I have seen the Muslim regimes empowering many billionaires overnight in the name of their brotherhood. They get the best and fattest of the contracts. All manner of preferences are manufactured to buttress their choice of the contractors. When the Christians are in charge opposite happens. The bondwoman's children do still call the shots even when their regime is out of power.

Why can't the Christian regimes select a few businessmen and empower them in the reminiscent manner? Not only that both the Christian regime and their brothers do act strangely against one another. Most vocal critics and protagonists of Christian governments are the so- called brothers of the same faith. Their attacks on the government will be very virulent that one may consider them as being hired to do so. Most of the times, from a balanced point of view, it will be certain that there is no basis for the antagonism.

I have had physical encounters with these agents of darkness in the marketplaces. There are many particular case studies when we encountered some hired marabous; which were paid heavily to speak continually to the heavens. They were asked to program through their evil prayers such things as confusion, costly and irredeemable mistakes on the part of the governor, president or Chief Executive Officer (CEO). These occult powers wield much economic influence and control the media houses. It is not difficult to escalate minor issues and blow them out of proportion.

Efficacy of Sacrifices and Cosmic Influence

Let me give every reader of this book an assignment. At midday (12 noon), please enter into a shop or business being owned and run by an Indian who worships one of their gods. You will notice the altar and incense being offered to their gods. In Mozambique, about 95% of all the businesses in that nation are controlled by the Indians. Therefore, at midday, serious sacrifices and burning of incense are heavily adhered to. It is usually a cloud of incense at noon in the major cities.

I was teaching in an East African country on the topic: **"Dealing with the influence of heavenly elements in the marketplace."** An electrical engineer, who had a contract with a big firm, met me after one of the sessions. He exclaimed with amazement, how his client (one of the operators of a chain store) in a shopping mall did something bizarre. He stated the following observation:

*On a particular day, a team of senior officers of the business arrived at the mall with some cans of fresh milk. They announced that they have sighted the **Pleiades**. Therefore, there must be an immediate opening ceremony for the chain store. They stated that if the store was not declared open within the next few days, they don't know when next the stars will appear in such a cluster soon. They exerted such undue pressure on the electrical contractor to hasten his work.*

The contractor stated that he renegotiated with them and worked with his team even at nights. He narrated that the executives of the business came with some strange fellows at one particular night with the fresh milk, spent almost the whole nights, speaking to the heavens and made some declarations. After my teachings of that night he explained that he has begun to understand the reasons why there is always unusual seduction of the masses towards the chain stores wherever they are situated.

They employ their priests even in corporate office to do the same for them. The Church should understand how far these guys could go in pursuit of wealth. They stop at nothing to get what they want. They help corrupt African politicians to export all their ill-gotten wealth to other nations of their choice for safe keeping.

A Need for Prayer Altars in our Establishments

Companies and parastatals should constitute prayer teams or even hire the services a minister and his team to take responsibility to pray for our companies always? There are strategic times and seasons that are set apart for such rituals. We need to have understanding of the times and seasons. This will enable us to deal with whatever they may have programmed into the heavens.

I have ministered to distressed companies and parastatals, which bounced back to life. There is a company which the director has been close to me, through the force of prayers, training and establishing covenant relationships with GOD, that company was turned around dramatically and it became one of the best of its kind in the city where I live. GOD wants us to transform everything around us through kingdom oriented training, discipleship and prayers.

Everything on this planet earth responds to the word of GOD. Start prophesying and speaking positive words to every company and business persons. You will marvel how quick they will start a progressive journey.

Mountain of Entertainment/Sports

The Holy Spirit gave me some wonderful explanations when I was in a deep meditative session. He began to download the mysteries behind great talents, gifts and callings of great men and women in the previous and present generations. For example, before GOD gave Israel a king, He gave them first of all a priest. There are certain families and individuals that had priestly heritage. But, before they could discover their gifts, Satan had already hijacked them for corrupt priestly service. Some had wonderful talents in singing but answered the call negatively. Apostle Paul said that in his zeal to serve the LORD, who called him he never knew he had answered the call in a corrupt way.

There are many mountains today where it is almost very difficult to call the name of the LORD there. To read the bible or pray looks like it's been outlawed. Sports men and women even those who go to Church cannot be bold to confess CHRIST on the mountain of sports.

Galatians 1:13-16 (NIV)
[13]For you have heard of my previous way of life in Judaism, how intensely I persecuted the church of God and tried to destroy it. [14]I was advancing in Judaism beyond many Jews of my own age and was extremely zealous for the traditions of my fathers. [15]But when God, who set me apart from birth and called me by his grace, was pleased [16]to reveal his Son in me so that I might preach him among the Gentiles,

These are the major reasons for creative exploits in entertainment industry in negative ways. People now use the GOD's given talent to exalt self or promote humanism. Through our compassionate priestly intercessions, they will be turned to the LORD at the appointed time.

These ones who have turned and those who will turn to the LORD will be the essential instrument in the hands of the LORD for a great harvest in the entertainment/

sports industry. The Church must train the men who will disciple these potential tools when they would have turned to the LORD. And many are doing so now. Would we allow them to be like sheep without shepherd? Beyond the training and the discipleship, we must understand how to redeem the redemptive gifts and harness them to the glory of GOD.

Mountain of Media

We must recognize that there is an organized confederacy of global media houses against the Church in almost all the countries of the world. There is this general hatred against the Church. The media house tends to unleash the reign of hatred to Christianity. The few Christian media houses are not focused on bringing their voices together through a strong cable network.

The Arabs have found a voice for expressing their agenda through the Aljazeera Cable Network. When shall the Church rend her voice to the world? We need to locate a window of opportunity to launch our own real media houses. We need to create a media house that will attract the world and cause them to listen to those things that interest them, give the world a balance/critical current affairs in a kingdom style and at the same time deliver the message of the kingdom of GOD to them.

Prayer Points

• Let us to ask GOD to reveal to us the rot in the whole mountain and give us the burden to cry out in repentance.

• This is the time to pray for the release of human capital that the LORD will use to harness the gains of the coming wealth transfer.

- Wealth and leadership must be transferred, baton must change hand; we need divine positioning in order to take over at the appointed time. Ask GOD to reposition you.

Chapter Thirteen

THE ROD OF ZION AND THE TEAM

I was handed a complimentary copy of a book titled the "Rod of Zion" by the author Dr. James Obeng, published by Dayspring Media House 2013.

When GOD called Gideon, he told him the He will use him to deliver Israel as one man.
Judges 6:16 (NKJV)
16And the Lord said to him, "Surely I will be with you, and you shall defeat the Midianites as one man."
God promised to defeat the Midianites through Gideon as one man. Yet, He chose to select a team of three hundred fighting men for Gideon. David's name was composed in a victorious song which provoked King Saul to jealousy. Yet, he built a formidable team of four hundred mighty men. This team was unequalled to any other team in the history of human conflicts of all times.

The mighty men of David had great and enviable qualification which no one would desire to hire in modern soldiering. Only a few could qualify to be inducted into French Foreign Legion. Please Google www.frenchforeignlegion.com.

1 Sam 22:1-2 (NIV)
¹David left Gath and escaped to the cave of Adullam. When his brothers and his father's household heard about it, they went down to him there. ²All those who were in distress or in debt or discontented gathered around him, and he became their leader. About four hundred men were with him.

These men were loved in their inadequacies, inabilities and shortcomings. David became their leader in the wilderness, cave and in famine. I considered their qualifications, contributions, dedications and consecration. I wondered that GOD could use a single individual to transform a host of such ex jail birds, distressed, discontented and grossly indebted fellows.
GOD.

Whenever their contributions to the nation's armed forces are mentioned, my heirs tend to react by standing erect. All of these men were unequaled in their exploits. Their solidarity to David and the nation was unquestionable. May GOD see you as a rod that will be sent out of Zion to rule in the midst of your enemies. Daniel, Joseph, Nehemiah and other great Jewish exiles and slaves did marvelously spectacular in their age, conquered their mountains and established the dominion in the name of the LORD on those hills. How can't you discover your mountain toady and begin to possess?

The Leader as the Rod of Zion

This proclamation of the Psalmist is an insight into how the LORD would raise an army that will take over the seven mountains. The time has come that we do not need to post men according to our hearth desires. We need to see through the eyes of GOD and how He had selected men of valor in sundry times and seasons.

Psalms 110:2-3 (NKJV)
²The Lord shall send the rod of Your strength out of Zion.

Rule in the midst of Your enemies!
[3]Your people shall be volunteers
In the day of Your power...

We have entered into the season of His power. Men will volunteer to be enlisted into this great emerging force. It is the LORD that will anoint the David in us as a rod that must be sent out. This rod will rule (subdue and establish dominion) in the midst of our enemies. The enemies are the occupants of the seven mountains. The volunteers are not going to create a separate mountain to influence, they will rule in the midst of the existing mountains. The remnant exiled Jews did yet those were not the days of manifesting the kingdom power as our generation has.

The Leader and His Team

One vital aspect of a person of influence is to be determined to create a difference. To be an agent of change, one needs not to be at the top to cause changes to happen. A proper agent of change can cause changes from any position including being at the security post of an organization. Mordecai was a slave at the security post of the king, yet he paid a great prize, made sacrifice and saved the Jewish race.

You may not be remembered as the one who did it. One thing is certain, heaven has taken record. There must be a day of remembrance. Mordecai was a man of substance he understood his genealogy. He knew his breed and that they are usually the agents of change everywhere they go. He understands that they can survive in any nation and make great things out of nothing.

Naaman was a great soldier, whom the LORD has given victories in diverse ways. It was a mere slave girl in his house that brought solution to his reproach of leprosy. If that slave girl had kept mute, it is possible that Naaman would have died of his leprosy.

2 Kings 5:2-3 (NIV)
²Now bands from Aram had gone out and had taken captive a young girl from Israel, and she served Naaman's wife. ³She said to her mistress, "If only my master would see the prophet who is in Samaria! He would cure him of his leprosy."

A Mountain and a Team of Adventurists

Pastors are the leading catalysts in this adventure. We must create prayer departments in our churches that will be in charge only to pray for Christian businesses and business men/women. We need to organize trainings, seminars and conferences specially designed to impart and impact on the business community of the brotherhood in our nations.

Any child of GOD in every organization should have a prayer schedule and strategy to pray in the organization and for the organization. It doesn't matter if the business is owned by heathen or not, GOD posted you there as a yeast, light and salt to bring positive change. He/she must identify fellow burden bearer in the same organization or disciple one through relationship. When I was working in a mega corporation, I imparted my department that my fame was known in many departments. The legacy I left cannot be wiped out easily. I was discoursing with a pastor, who worked there some years back, (after I had left). I told him that I also had worked there, before his redeployment. He exclaimed and told me that almost everybody was commending the exploits I did in that department.

One major sacrifice was my break time. I gave it up for prayers. I had other like-minded fellows from other departments, who linked up with me, in the lunch hour fellowship. I taught everyone that there is no special time to pray. While working or walking in or out of office, speak to GOD in prayers. I also taught them that everyone that works both with papers, instruments or equipment; should know and understand that everything obeys the command of the words of GOD in prayers.

One of my colleagues who were a plant manager was promoted for excellence in his department. He told me that he used to speak to and command the machines never to break down. Oftentimes, he would anoint them with oil and command them to work without breaking down. The contractors whom were in charge of maintaining the machines were angry with him without a cause. They were thrown out the job because there was nothing to maintain.

We must demonstrate the kingdom power in every part of the mountains. We will rule by the power in the word of GOD. We can regulate the mechanisms of plants. We can determine accurately where the mineral are deposited. We can predict accurately the position of the global stock exchange. We can control the election pendulum in the direction of the GOD of heavens. We can identify incoming great opportunities.

We need to be on our duty post as Daniel in order to cause a revolution. The revolution is coming. And now, is the time to arise and go with these our might. We must discover our wings. We must discover our talents. We must discover our calling. We must discover our offices. We must discover our weaknesses and our strengths. We must discover to recover our lost heritages.

Prayer Points

- Rod and scepters are symbol of authority, pray and ask GOD to make you a scepter and authority in His hand for contest on the seven mountains.

- Pray GOD to make you victorious in all the battles on the mountains.

- Proclaim that the mountains will bow and the hills will bow before you.

- Declare that the mountain of the LORD's house will be established on all the mountains and the hills and every man shall bow before it.

- In the day of GOD's power, I will be a volunteer in JESUS name.

Chapter Fourteen

STRATEGIC HIGH LEVEL SPIRITUAL WARFARE

Cosmic Level Conflicts

Once again spiritual warfare is defined as the conflict between the kingdom of darkness and the kingdom of light. The conflict is all about which of the kingdom is in control of ruler ship, resources, souls of men and the universe **(Source: PMTI Syllabus 2001)**.

When we talk about strategic high level conflict; we are trying to explain specialized and deep dimension of tactical spiritual warfare. Which simply mean, deeper dimension of prayers that are targeted at certain times and seasons. These prayers are understood as spiritual warfare because they are organized to combat the powers and influence of the kingdom of darkness. These powers operate in the heavenly realms.

These types of prayer are mostly targeted at dealing with the controlling influence of heavenly elements such as: moon, sun and stars. These controlling influences have ever since been the focal point of the kingdom of darkness. They have exhibited this art since medieval times to the utmost disadvantages of the Church. This level of understanding which the LORD has brought to the Church is to enable us not only to contend with them but to have dominion in all the mountains of influence.

The following scripture explained that there is spiritual wickedness in the high (heavenly places):

Ephesians 6:12 (NIV)

[12]*For our struggle is not against flesh and blood, but against the rulers, against the authorities, against the powers of this dark world and against the <u>spiritual forces of evil in the heavenly realms</u>.*

Ephesians 6:12 (NKJV)

[12]*For we do not wrestle against flesh and blood, but against principalities, against powers, against the rulers of the darkness of this age,* against spiritual hosts of wickedness in the <u>heavenly places</u>.*

These spiritual hosts of wickedness or spiritual forces of wickedness do operate in the heavenly **places** or heavenly **realms**, all are in plurals. It is very plane that they are operating in the first and the second realms of the heavens. In the third realm or third heaven, they don't have the capabilities to function there. Why does the bible call it spiritual wickedness? It is because they are jealously in control of the political and economic destinies of the seven mountains. In their dominion and control, any perceived incursion is destroyed mercilessly. Consider the visitation of the wise men to the infant JESUS. In Revised Standard Version (RSV) of the bible, it is rendered the Magi. This is derived from Greek word magic. Therefore, the wise men, magicians or astrologers; who visited JESUS were not Jews. They specialize in star gazing or reading and interpreting the stars (star gazers).

They may have probably tried to hijack the prophetic destiny of the Baby. When they may have tried several times in futility, they decided to pay homage to the owner of such star. Have you ever considered the mysteries behind the three powerful gifts? The Gold, Frankincense

123

and Myrrh were highly symbolic. Gold reserve of a nation is the measure of that nation's wealth. Frankincense is symbolic as its name frank or pure incense. Incense is a symbol of worship. Myrrh is a symbol of expensive fragrance. It is one of the most essential ingredients in compounding the olive oil. It is also a measure of splendor or glory.

Therefore, the wise men/astrologers/star gazers surrendered to the LORD JESUS all the wealth, all the worship and all the glory, anointing and power unto Him. That was the appointed time to surrender whatever they have been wrongly in control for generations. And I prophesy that this is our time of repossessing the seven mountains. Whatever the enemy has been possessing wrongly shall be released in JESUS name. We must dethrone them and be enthroned.

To explain the whole of this topic of conflicts with the heavenly elements in this chapter will be a great trial. I am thinking of a separate treatise. However, I will be pleased to state that we can wage wars through the stars. We can deploy or charge the stars to fight for us. We can destabilize the things programed or fastened into the elements of heavens by the occult men. I advise you to get a copy of *"Waging War with the Stars"* (**Dr. Steve Ogan, 2013**).

Deborah Made a Prayer
Judges 5:20-21 (NIV)
²⁰From the heavens the stars fought, from their courses they fought against Sisera.
²¹The river Kishon swept them away, the age-old river, the river Kishon.

This song by Prophetess Deborah was an illustration on how she incited or commanded the stars to fight against the enemy of Israel. The stars fought in their order or courses. As they began to fight, the rivers responded and fought together alongside the stars.

There are certain times, days and seasons that are more strategic than other periods. JESUS was not to remain on the cross beyond the special Sabbath day or high day. Thus, He was crucified on the first day of the first month. To signify that He has fulfilled His purpose as the supreme and the last sacrificial Passover lamb that takes away the sins of the world.

John 19:31 (NKJV)
[31]Therefore, because it was the Preparation Day, that the bodies should not remain on the cross on the Sabbath (for that Sabbath was a high day),

There is a lamentation in the bible where JESUS bemoaned that the children of this world are in this generation wiser than the children of the kingdom.

Luke 16:8 (NKJV)
[8]For the sons of this world are more shrewd in their generation than the sons of light.

May we be more prudent and shrewd more than the sons of light in all our generations than the children of the world! The bible has declared that we are the light of the world and the salt of the earthy (Mat. 5:13-14). There are two great questions in these two quoted scriptures. If the salt loses its virtue is it not good for nothing? And can a candle be lit and be hidden in a bushel? The answer is never!

Strategic Times and Seasons

The following are some of the strategic times and seasons that are constant. The kingdom of darkness is more concerned on what must be done at the gates of these times than at other times of the year.

Summer solstice
Winter solstice
Autumnal Equinox and
Vernal Equinox

Others are certain movements of the heavenly elements such as the eclipse, New and Full Moon periods, first and last quarter of the moon etc.

Luminous strategies of the illuminati and the Freemasons

From the ancient time till now, men have devised certain strange and strategic ways of taking undue advantage of the greater population of mankind. Satan on his side has been covenanted by these few who had to pay great sacrifices to be enabled. Ancient tombs and monuments have been discovered as some of the strategic strongholds and altars of sacrifice for such transcendental prognostications.

2 Corinthians 11:14-15 (NIV)
[14]And no wonder, for Satan himself masquerades as an angel of light. [15]It is not surprising, then, if his servants masquerade as servants of righteousness.

These cultic organizations as mentioned above have mastered the secret arts of using witchcraft to conjure and control lives and events to the utmost advantages of their membership. At strategic times, they do offer terrible sacrifices ranging from human beings, fattened livestock, and huge sums of money or properties. Thus, they pay such prizes and offer enormous sacrifices at such specific times to prevail on all the mountains. Thereafter, (with the sacrifices) their priests are hired to speak into the heavens, fasten their names, companies or products at such strategic gates or beginning of times. The major reason is to have domineering influence and control of such things they desire through the help of these luminous elements in the heavens.

As they program and fasten their names upon the heavenly elements, those names are tied to these constellations to receive illumination or lights. These lights are thereafter caused to shine, attract and influence the programed names into the heart of the populace in the same way the light does into the universe. Their names, products, produce and works attracts undue patronages that are not measurable.

Genesis 1:14-19 (NIV)
[14]And God said, "Let there be lights in the expanse of the sky to separate the day from the night, and let them serve as signs to mark seasons and days and years, [15]and let them be lights in the expanse of the sky to give light on the earth." And it was so. [16]God made two great lights — the greater light to govern the day and the lesser light to govern the night. He also made the stars. [17]God set them in the expanse of the sky to give light on the earth, [18]to govern the day and the night, and to separate light from darkness. And God saw that it was good. [19] And there was evening, and there was morning—the fourth day.

There are two great lights, which GOD created, namely; the greater and the lesser lights. Notice that charge was given to the greater light to rule the day while the lesser rules the night. Scientists told us that all the hosts of heavens derive their lights from the greater light (the sun).

No wonder most so-called successful men and women are members of the Illuminati organization. Almost all the influential politicians, trendy socialites, musicians, and mega and multinational companies subscribe to their membership. One major force of their stock in trade is to cast spells of darkness (at strategic times) to any perceived competing person, product or parastatal, in order, to bring such entity out of relevance.

We have encountered their agents which were hired to carry out such nefarious transactions at the gate of times and to make some negative declarations against some Christian establishments. I have personally arrested one at the road leading to the church where I worship. That was a decisive period when we were in a twenty four hour nonstop chain prayers. Don't be deceived, the kingdom of darkness knows whenever something spectacular is about to happen in a territory. They have their own demonic intelligence network.

Should we pretend that nothing like this is happening? It does, it is still happening and will still be until the Churches rises up to say no to those things through strategic prayers and intercessions. How do we deal with those things? The answer will be found in the following concluding chapter.

Prayer Points

- Start by bringing repentance on all the wickedness in worshiping and covenanting with the powers of the heavenly bodies.

- In whichever way you are directly or indirectly connected, ask GOD for mercy.

- Appropriate the blood of JESUS into the sun, moon, stars, and the whole heavenly elements to blot out every spoken word that entrenched the agents of Satan over the mountains.

- Nullify through the blood of JESUS various covenants made with heavenly elements by the agents of darkness to control destinies and businesses.

- Command the luminous influences of the kingdom of darkness and their organizations to be darkened.

- Speak into the moon, sun, stars and other elements, command all that are programmed over them by the cultists to wither.

- Command the great hail stones from heaven to descend and destroy all their structures, strongholds and altars of the wicked (Josh. 10:10-11).

- Command their negative influences over your personal life, marriage, business and carrier to be blotted out in JESUS name.

- Command your star to shine brighter and brighter every day.

- Declare that the light and the glory of the LORD will arise upon you and overflow upon the seven mountains.

- Ask GOD to dethrone the heathen and enthrone the righteous.

- Proclaim that you shall radiate and be seen as the star of JESUS in the East.

EPILOGUE

The contest on the mount should be an organized struggle. The struggle to unseat the enemies on the Seven Mountains should be concerted, consistent and persistent. No one goes to the battle without preparations, strategies and logistics. We need to pull our knowledge resources together. To do so, a proper spiritual mapping needs to be assessed by spiritual cartographers. The topography of the Mountains is strategic in propagating the strategic warfare. The principalities that dwell respectively on the mountain must be discerned and deposed. GOD told the children of Israel; '... that I have given into thine hand Sihon the Amorite, king of Heshbon, and his land: begin to possess it, and contend with him in battle. This day will I begin to put the dread of thee and the fear of thee upon the nations that are under the whole heaven, who shall hear report of thee, and shall tremble, and be in anguish because of thee'.

Secondly, GOD spoke to Jeremiah:

Jeremiah 1:9-10 (KJV)
⁹Then the Lord put out his hand and touched my mouth. And the Lord said to me,
"Behold, I have put my words in your mouth.
 ¹⁰See, I have set you this day over nations and over kingdoms,
 to pluck up and to break down,
to destroy and to overthrow,
to build and to plant."

In spite of, the land of the Amorites being given to the Israelis, they had two pronged approaches; they are:

to possess it and contend with them in battle. GOD's own responsibilities are two folds: put the dread of Israel and their fear against the Amorites. Then the Amorites will also know two things: they will tremble and be in anguish.

Furthermore, GOD has put His words in our mouth, set us as prophets over the mountains of nations and kingdoms; to exercise His mandate and dominion; to pluck up, break down, destroy and overthrow. Thereafter, we shall BUILD and PLANT the kingdom structures and infrastructures on those mountains.

Drawing an insight in the book, Seven Mountain Prophecies by Jonny Enlow, who classified with understanding from other Seven Mountains expositors; some of the powers that govern the mountains as we will see shortly.

Every church/ministry organization must set up a prayer department, whose duty is to pray for those in business or workplaces. They are to travail for the emergence of kingdom power brokers on the Seven Mountains. These teams must be volunteers, those who are burdened to intercede. They must comprise of the five-fold ministers and be filled with the whole nine or more gifts of the HOLY SPIRIT.

Their responsibilities could be drawn from this scripture:
Isaiah 62:6-7 (KJV)
⁶I have set watchmen upon thy walls, O Jerusalem, which shall never hold their peace day nor night: ye that make mention of the Lord, keep not silence,
⁷And give him no rest, till he establish, and till he make Jerusalem a praise in the earth.

We need to know and understand that prayer is a project. Therefore, we must give our Watchmen/ Intercessors these guidelines:

1.   Watchmen/Intercessors must be set up for the combat on the mountains.

2.   They must be continuous, concerted and consistent prayers day and night (Unbroken chain prayers).

3.   We need to give our GOD no rest.

4.   Until, He establishes and makes the Seven Mountains a possession of the LORD for the Ecclesia on the earth.

I.   Mountain of the Hittites called the MEDIA Mountain

The principality that rules on this mountain is called Apollyon. It has tail as scorpion which by interpretation is known as Fear, terror or distortion. The Ecclesia - the called out ones must contend with them in battles. They are to be deposed before the eventual possession.

II.   Mountain of the Girgasites called the GOVERNMENT Mountain

The principality that rules on this mountain is Lucifer his major characteristics is oppression, control and manipulation.

III.   Mountain of the Amorites also known as EDUCATION

Its major characteristics are pride and humanism. The ruling principality is Serpent. The serpent knew the truth and went with a different sermon and convinced Adam and Eve that the forbidden fruit will bring knowledge of good and evil.

IV.   **Mountain of the Canaanite called the ECONOMY Mountain**
The ruling spirit is Mammon or Babylon. This mountain is also a decisive mountain. The contest for economic power via acquisition of overwhelming wealth leads men to more dastard acts against humanity.

V.   **Perizzites Mountain known as the RELIGIOUS Mountain**
The principal spirit on this mountain is called, Beelzebub or Baal. This is the focal point of this treatise. This is the mountain that is above all the mountains. This is the mountain that can depose or dethrone other mountains. And afterwards be enthroned, exalted and established above all other mountains and hills.

VI.   **Hivites Mountain. ENTERTAINMENT and SPORTS Mountain**
The principal spirit is Jezebel. This spirit is responsible for the rot and corruption in the entertainment and sports industries.

VII.   **Mountain of the Jebusites. FAMILY Mountain**
The principal spirit is Marin Spirit. All over the world, it's been proven on research statistics that all the regions (coastal areas on the earth) are places of massive distortion to family values and virtues. In these regions, divorces and single parentages are on the increase than other vicinities.

We need to know the strategic times and seasons of the year. We must download the annual calendars of solstices, equinoxes, Halloween, eclipses and lunar calendars. We must not allow the enemies to out pray us in these seasons. These are the seasons in which they offer great sacrifices for their perpetuation on the seven mountains. Also, we must key into some major Jewish festivals to harness the spiritual importance of those festivities.

Things to Pray and Deal With:

COVENANTS
The kingdom of darkness understands the word covenants more than the Church. They do nothing without a covenant with their master. These covenants will be annulled.

SACRIFICES
There are certain sacrifices which the enemy may present as a token of argument before GOD. Therefore we will present the supreme sacrifice of the blood of JESUS to overturn theirs.

PRIESTHOOD
We must terminate the satanic priesthood that had been leading the occupant of the mountains. Thereafter, we will enthrone the priesthood of our LORD JESUS whereby we will rule and rein as kings and priests on the earth (Rev. 1:6).

AGENTS AND AGENCIES
In addition to the above mentioned principal spirits, we must execute judgment of GOD against the agents of the kingdom of darkness and their agencies.

As we do these and many more which the HOLY SPIRIT will lead and reveal to us. We can be getting ready for a great harvest in the market or public places.

ABOUT THE AUTHOR

Apostle Joe Paul is called into the Ministry of Intercession, Missions and Deliverance. He has traveled to over 30 countries ministering with signs and wonders. He is currently on the board of Trustees of Pastors/Ministers Prayer Network, International. He has been privileged to minister in many national and international conferences, seminars and workshops. He is highly sought after in deliverance and breakthrough ministrations.

He is also a trained Shipping and Transport Consultant and a Member of Certified International Trade Logistics (CITLS).

Apostle Joe ministers with passion on strategic spiritual warfare handling; both deliverance to individuals, families, cities and nations with great power of the Holy Ghost. He is a great asset in teaching, training and discipleship programs to ministers, churches and professionals of diverse fields. He has also written other literary works, in addition to this one, which includes; the book entitled: "The Power and Influence of Altars."

He is happily married to Elizabeth and they are blessed with two lovely Children (a girl and a boy) Flourish and Summit. They both live in Port Harcourt, Nigeria.

For further inquiries, contact the author.

Joe Paul
+2348033411858, +2347089629052
E-mail: pastor_josephpaul@yahoo.com,
         archpope.pmpn@gmail.com.

www.ingramcontent.com/pod-product-compliance
Lightning Source LLC
La Vergne TN
LVHW022011080426
835513LV00009B/674